ADVANCE PRAISE

"This is a powerful book, a breakthrough on the power of empathy and connection in doing the essential work of selling possibility and hope."

—**Seth Godin**, best-selling author, *This Is Marketing*

"David A. Smith has written an extremely important and practical book that should be a must-read for all senior living professionals, not just those involved in marketing and sales. With more than 30 years of success as an owner, operator, and consultant, Smith provides the reader with unique and profound insights about our customers. This book will enlighten all, even those who have worked in the profession for many years who think they understand all they need to know about selling to seniors."

—**David Schless**, President, American Seniors
Housing Association, Washington, DC

"David Smith is a giant in the senior living sales space. He invented Prospect-Centered Selling (PCS) to show our industry how to sell people a product they really didn't want, and I mean REALLY didn't want, but one they desperately needed. Because of Prospect-Centered Selling, we improved our sales closing ratios, and our sales consultants found a new fondness for the sales process. It gave our sales consultants purpose. David insisted that we connect and build trust before offering solutions. Above all, we shouldn't rush the process, because trust is built over time, and trust is the secret sauce to senior living sales success."

—**Richard Westin**, CEO, Agemark,
San Francisco, CA

"I am an owner and COO of Charter Senior Living. I was first introduced to David years ago at a national conference. His concept was to invest more time with prospects, doing home visits, creative follow-ups, and aligning with the prospect. It was different than any other sales approach, and at the time David was perceived as a rebel in the industry. Many executives just couldn't make a paradigm switch to PCS. I took a leap of faith and adopted PCS. I have never looked back. I brought Prospect-Centered Selling everywhere I went and within three to four months, I saw increases in sales conversions and move-ins. Communities that were averaging two to three move-ins per month were able to nearly double their results. I want to thank David for never giving up on his vision. With this book, his tenaciousness and desire to change the way we sell in senior housing is coming to fruition. I now hear many organizations talking about Time in The Selling Zone, home visits, case studies, and creative follow-ups. You did it, David. You changed the way we are all selling in the industry."

—**Jayne Sallerson**, Partner, Chief Operating
Officer, Charter Senior Living, Boston, MA

"David is a visionary in the senior housing field. I had the pleasure of working in the trenches to learn from him while he filled communities in both Chicago and Texas over 20 years ago. Since then, I have incorporated many of his philosophies and techniques into my own consulting and coaching style. I highly recommend his sales approach and his book."

—**Kristin Kutac Ward**, Founder and CEO,
Solutions Advisors and Solvere, Saint Petersburg, FL

"When I'm working with sales professionals who may feel stuck in advancing prospects toward making a senior living move-in decision, I recommend slowing down to win more often. Taking the time to understand a prospective resident and their family's level of readiness, including emotional readiness, enables the sales-person to offer personalized next steps in line with the customer's needs. Knowing more does take time, leveraging the knowledge gained will increase the likelihood of welcoming new residents to your senior living community. The PCS process David A. Smith discusses in this book has impacted my coaching conversations, which have affected the experiences of the prospective residents and their families talking with our sales teams. This book will help your sales teams understand how slowing down doesn't mean going slow."

—**Kelly Singleton-Meyers**, SVP of Sales,
Sunrise Senior Living, Cleveland, OH

"David Smith is a true pioneer in senior living sales. The introduction of Prospect-Centered Selling into an industry driven by obsolete, transactional sales methods not only changed the way we looked at sales in the senior living sector, but it also drastically improved the results of those who adopted this methodology. It not only improves sales performance in the US but in Canada as well. Presenting the background and theory of this approach in *It's About Time!* provides a practical opportunity for all of us to learn more from David!"

—**Jason Moorehead**, Vice President of Sales and
Marketing, Revera Retirement, Ontario, Canada

"I met David Smith while I was searching to find a sales system that was complementary to my trademarked system, 'The WOW! Experience'. My system focused on the complex process that teaches how to nurture and advance a connection with the potential customer. But I needed more depth, clarity, and training tools for my teams. There were a lot of sales systems out there, but nothing else that focused on the lives and journeys of our prospects and families. David and PCS taught people how to dive deep through empathetic listening and a guided approach that would help them be better salespeople. I have watched David's approach help our sales teams become much more effective and increase their success rates. It has helped us at a time when competition is at an all-time high and, of course, as we bear the added stress of a global pandemic. I'm fortunate to call David a colleague and a friend who shares my passion for helping seniors and their families find solutions in a complex world."

—**Kevin Carlin**, MS, Principal,
Meridian Senior Living, Bethesda, MD

"I was captivated after hearing David Smith present at a national conference. He spoke about what to do with a prospect or family member who came to check it out but wasn't sure whether a move was in their best interests. I found it refreshing to hear someone address that critical issue. His Prospect-Centered Selling methodology soon became the governing sales technique of our company. Now, 20 years later, Balfour has continued to use this innovative and still unique approach to sales and marketing, and its occupancy at all communities consistently exceeds that of its competitors by 5 to 10 percent, averaging consistently 95 to 100 percent."

—**Michael Schonbrun**, Founder and CEO,
Balfour Senior Living, Louisville, CO

"We had learned about PCS from David Smith and years ago made it part of our culture. His exciting new book, along with the Sherpa CRM, empowers us to guide the behavior of our sales professionals in a much more focused and precise way. With PCS, our overall average visit to move-in closing ratio went up by 50 percent, which is an incredible achievement. I believe the late Tony Mullen, one of our industry's pioneers, who co-founded the NIC. Tony said that David and PCS will revolutionize the industry forever. We agree. This book lays out how you can join the senior living sales revolution."

—**Jason Rock**, Seniors Housing/Active Adult Sales and
Marketing, Allegro Senior Living, Palm City, FL

"Prospect-Centered Selling has been instrumental in the success of my senior living career over the last 15 years. David's approach to PCS honors and values the genuine relationships that our sales teams build with prospective residents in guiding their decision to make a transformational change in their lives for the better. In this book, David offers a simple but proven formula for helping resistant prospects 'get ready,' connect empathically, untangle emotional resistance, then advance toward 'ready' in small steps. The foundations of PCS in this book will not only improve your occupancies but will also improve how you communicate as a team and as a leader."

—**Jacqueline Omstead**, Director of Operations and Sales, PARC Retirement Communities, Vancouver, Canada

"Generations' transition to Prospect-Centered Selling was strategic and mission-driven. 'Enhancing Lives and Celebrating the Excitement of Living' is a mission statement we work to live out in all aspects of our business. Upon learning more about the PCS scientific and measurable approach, along with the focus on 'relationship' rather than 'closing,' we were all in. What we have learned in these past years is that it has been a 'road less traveled' experience. Shifting out of old industry habits of selling, changing our mindset (we do have enough leads), and deepening our belief that with this strategy, we not only could get to 100 percent occupancy but maintain high occupancy took time. It also took a deep commitment from owners, community leadership, and sales staff. Like the flywheel concept, once Sherpas made meaningful traction on quality advances, with thoughtful CFU and more than adequate Time in The Selling Zone, magic happened. We found companywide that our residents were more satisfied and engaged and had longer stays, and PCS helped feed an otherwise already healthy community culture.

I can't say enough about David's work and the impact on us at Generations. I am very grateful for him and how his work is shifting our industry focus to where it should be: on our prospects."

—**Melody Gabriel**, CEO, Generations, Portland, OR

"David and his team have done an incredible job in developing the Prospect-Centered Selling process. PCS brings our sales and marketing people back to a time that was truly 'primal' in its approach. The entire premise of the approach is based on developing a relationship with the prospect that enjoys a foundation of trust. Trust, as we all know, in a sales environment, is like Pandora's box, as it opens the most important phase of the sales process: discovery! This process enables our team to truly facilitate the desires of our prospects in the most expedient way possible, ultimately helping the team exceed the expectations of our prospects time and time again."

—**Kevin Pidgeon**, President, Nautical Lands
Group of Companies, Ontario, Canada

"I have a lot of fond and scary memories about the early days of trying to fill the Breakers at Edgewater Beach. It was my first and flagship community, and getting it filled really led to my success today, thanks to David and his selling style. What really separates David and Prospect-Centered Selling from other selling approaches is that they do things that are outrageous and outside of the box. That's what makes it exciting. David truly likes what he does and the people he works with. Everything is done as a team approach, and everyone has fun doing it!"

—**William Kaplan**, Chairman of the Board,
Senior Lifestyle Corporation, Chicago, IL

"For those of us in the emerging UK senior living market, this book is fascinating. Generally, the sector here has a long way to go to move away from the real estate approach, and we are working on it! Reading about the history of senior living in this book, it was heartening to see that we're not the only ones struggling to evolve to a person-centered perspective. When it comes to retirement communities, the UK has a lot to learn from the US. Especially from pioneers such as David Smith, who throughout this book reminds us to focus on what customers really want—instead of what we think they need."

—**Michael Voges**, Executive Director, Associated Retirement
Community Operators UK (ARCO), London

"Connecting with David and learning his principles of PCS was a pivotal moment for our company, and also for me personally. Similar to his own personal experience referenced in the opening pages of the book, we were so focused on generating leads and 'selling' that we rarely took the time to slow down and listen to what our prospects were saying. Not only did a shift to a Prospect-Centered Selling approach allow us to achieve and maintain 100 percent occupancy, but it also allowed us to enhance our culture and services within our communities because we better understand those we are serving."

—**Greg C. Joyce**, Legacy Retirement Communities

"David has done so much for the senior housing and care industry. People like David are the reason it's so gratifying to work in this field! We met when I was the Director of External Relations with UMBC's Erickson School of Aging Studies, Executive Education Program. David was the lead instructor for the Sales and Marketing course. His approach was empathic and innovative. He taught that connecting deeply makes an extraordinary difference in helping people find their own motivation to move. In my current position, our nonprofit culture and mission focuses on teaching and advocacy for professionals who deeply care for seniors. This book will help you understand how adopting Prospect-Centered Selling is a natural path to higher occupancies and an extension of your company's mission. I give it my very highest recommendation!"

—**Kevin Heffner**, President, LifeSpan Network, Columbia, MD

"David, I want to tell you how much I appreciate your efforts to help me make the decision to move to The Gatesworth. Although I was reluctant at first, you and your team were very warm and engaging. It was obvious that they cared a lot about me as a person. Making the move was absolutely the best thing I ever did for myself and for my family. My only regret is that I didn't move sooner. The next time a prospect tells you that they aren't ready yet, please ask them for me: it's time. What are you waiting for?"

—**Ruth**, Resident, St. Louis, MO

IT'S ABOUT
TIME!

HOW TO GROW REVENUE
WITH PROSPECT-CENTERED
SELLING

DAVID A. SMITH

LIONCREST
PUBLISHING

IT'S ABOUT TIME!
How to Grow Revenue with Prospect-Centered Selling

ISBN 978-1-5445-2051-3 *Hardcover*
      978-1-5445-2050-6 *Paperback*
      978-1-5445-2049-0 *Ebook*
      978-1-5445-2052-0 *Audiobook*

I dedicate this book to my parents,
Phil and Gerry Smith. They inspired me to always strive
to be heroic and to make the world a better place.

To my in-laws, **David and Helen Spitzberg**, for their love,
support, and for their confidence to invest in me and The Gatesworth.
Also, to my bonus parent, **Vita von der Lancken**, and to
thousands of other older adults like her who "got ready" for a move
to senior living. People who courageously opened their hearts
and shared their life stories along with their fears and aspirations.
People who allowed me the honor to connect, assist in, and
guide their efforts to untangle resistance and then
advance toward a vibrant new lifestyle.

I further dedicate my book to those
Senior Living Sales Professionals who have adopted
a Prospect-Centered Sales approach. Professionals who motivate
and inspire transformation by respecting autonomy and
by understanding that prospects need our time and our personal
engagement. Time to build trust and to create a safe space to explore
their resistance to change. All this before considering solutions.
Along with the older adults who choose to
become residents, they are my heroes!

CONTENTS

FOREWORD

Alex Fisher, President/Co-founder,
Sherpa, www.sherpacrm.com

We *really* need a shift in the way we sell senior living, now more than ever. This book is being published amid the COVID-19 pandemic, the impact of which will be felt for years to come. It's a crisis that has had a direct impact on the senior living industry, amplifying many of the concerns, fears, and objections our prospective residents already had about the product we sell.

Within these pages, David shows us that, to successfully convert more prospects, our focus should be and should always have been on the *prospect*, not the *product*. And he's right. It's a concept backed by years of experience in the field. That is where the fill and turnaround teams he led consistently converted 50 percent or more of prospects that they got face to face with, increasing occupancies at dozens of communities across the US and Canada by 25 percent or more, usually with 90- to 120-day fill campaigns. It is also supported by a growing body of senior living sales data comparing a traditional sales approach to what we call Prospect-Centered Selling.

What we can hope comes of the coronavirus outbreak is real change and innovation, which I believe is crucial for our industry. And like our prospects themselves, those in the industry who made a much-needed change to their selling approach *before* a crisis have been in a much better situation to get through it.

Our prospective senior living customers have always demanded a lot more of us when it comes to sales. They need transparency, empathy, authenticity, and proof that we really understand them and want to help solve their problems. What we need is a way to integrate this prospect-centered approach with an actionable, measurable methodology that increases sales performance while delivering a better experience to our prospects before, during, and after the sale.

This book and the techniques within are not about quick tips, scripts, or the latest selling fad. Instead, you'll be immersed in a science-based, experience-born, results-oriented methodology that has been proven to build and sustain higher occupancies. It does this while also establishing a true market differentiator: your community is interested, above all, in what's best for your prospects and residents. And they feel the difference every step of the way.

I first saw these methods in action when David hired me at one of his communities, The Gatesworth, 20 years ago. I was new to the industry and started out in sales support. Little did I know, working with David would launch a meaningful and successful career for me and many others in senior living sales. In hindsight, I was very lucky; I would not have lasted long in the industry had I experienced the "accepted" sales approach of the time, which is still around today. It was a product-centered method where you "hit the hot buttons and tried for the tour/close." Or worse, you would do nothing and wait for people to call in who "really need us."

That was not the case at The Gatesworth. David, an owner-operator as well as hands-on sales leader, showed us that in order to succeed, we needed to focus on the prospect above all else. His instruction was simple: talk to them and learn about them. Right away, I was hooked. Rather than counting calls or tours, I would spend time with incredible human beings and engage in conversations rich with experiences and complexities. We would then work together as a team to figure out how we could best guide this person through the change they needed—but very often didn't want—to make. In terms of sales performance, David worked with us and with prospects. We were wildly successful with any senior living care type, community size, region, or financial structure. We also had an immense sense of accomplishment in inspiring older adults to live better lives.

David taught those who were fortunate to work with him what "being a hero with purpose" means. We wouldn't sit around and wait for the rare opportunity for heroism, like jumping in a river to save a drowning person. Instead, we would bring our heroic selves in a daily practice of grit, focus, and determination to achieve extraordinary results for ourselves and our prospects.

Time and time again, at countless industry conferences and consulting engagements, David would go against the grain and buck the accepted norms. I watched him introduce the concepts of measuring time as a qualitative measure of sales engagement. He would evangelize home visits, creative follow-up, and other breakthrough concepts that are now more widely accepted in senior living sales. He spent countless days, nights, and weekends deep in research or in the "sales trenches" of struggling communities that would rely on his ability to drive results, which he delivered.

As a senior living industry leader, regardless of your role, you have a big, difficult job. It's a task that requires nothing more, and nothing less, than a thorough understanding of your customer and the intention to do right by them. Be an advocate for your prospect's happiness and well-being, and you'll both see the rewards.

It's time to be a hero with purpose. You can do it, and this book will help guide you.

INTRODUCTION

E ver notice that some things just take time? When you bake a cake, you set out all the ingredients: flour, eggs, baking powder, milk, vanilla, salt, and butter. You can tweak the recipe, but the preparation time stays the same. You can't make twice as many cakes by baking each one half as long.

Time is also necessary and often inflexible when it comes to making significant, life-changing decisions. These are situations where someone needs to let go of the world as they've come to know it, like grieving, divorce, addiction, smoking cessation, etc. The decision-maker often has all the facts they need for a logical decision. No matter. Each needs time to identify, confront, and overcome their own emotional resistance to change.

For older adults considering a move to senior living, especially the higher-functioning individuals[1] who aren't forced to move due to a medical emergency, the decisions of whether, when, and where to move are absolutely life-changing and need to be made at their own pace. That's the lifestyle transition that I have studied: how to help senior adults accept the idea of change. We adapted practices from innovative approaches to complex sales and from extensive clinical research into readiness done by change psychologists. Embedded in the prospect-centered approach we have developed are strategies

---

[1] As used herein, "higher-functioning" is a relative term that refers to IL and AL residents who require little or no ongoing assistance with activities of daily living. For example, despite a variety of illnesses, prospects Ed and Rozine are ambulatory and require no medication management and no assistance with other activities of daily living. Rozine still drives, and both are still involved with outside community activities.

and approaches that can be applied to any complex, emotion-laden decision.

This book focuses on the decision to move into a senior living community. I love senior living and what it does to extend and enhance the lives of its residents. Achieving and maintaining 100 percent occupancy is critical to the wellness, socialization, and overall satisfaction of our residents, our prospects, and their respective family members.

Getting full is also critical for the financial viability of every senior living community. Today, there are roughly 25,000 senior housing vacancies in the US (10 percent of available units), representing about $100 million of lost revenue opportunity per month. Eliminating the lost opportunity cost of this vacancy is the single highest revenue-generating opportunity that most providers have. Getting full increases bottom-line cash flows and overall project value at sale or refinancing. Getting and staying full opens up opportunities to increase rates and enhance or expand programs and amenities. For a typical 100-unit community that has been open for more than a year, getting full only requires about 10 to 15 additional residents. Given the thousands of age- and income-qualified prospects in a typical primary market area, you don't need to close very many to get full. Yet anyone who has ever tried knows that senior living is very difficult to sell. It is a complex sale with an overlay of emotional resistance. You can make this complex sales process easier (less difficult), but you can't really make it simpler.

My first attempt to fill a senior living community was in 1988. I was going broke and at my wit's end trying to get to 100 percent occupancy at The Gatesworth. It was one of the very first purpose-built, upscale rental independent living (IL) communities. The concept was based on the idea that older adults who could afford it would welcome a resident-centered experience with wonderful food, beautiful venues, and ongoing opportunities for socialization. My partners and I launched our first phase with 220 apartments, large enough to support the robust staff and pro-gramming that we envisioned. We thought that if we built an incredible service-enriched environment, reasonably priced and in a great location, the prospects would come, fall in love, and close themselves.

My role was to find, qualify, pitch, and convert 220 prospects into residents as quickly as possible. We started pre-marketing a full year before opening. We spent a lot of money on direct mail, print ads, out-reach to community leaders, and a variety of educational and social events. We made cold calls off of purchased lists. Aside from working with investors and updating projections, I spent most of my time focused on new lead generation. My only purposeful "selling" or "conversion" strategy for my team of two full-time leasing counselors was to qualify new inquiries in terms of health, financial capacity, and urgency. Then, giving priority to the most urgent, we would try to entice them to tour as quickly as possible. The general message was: "Come see what we built for you. You are going to love it!" We didn't really consider much about the buyer's emotional state or their decision-making process. Rather, we envisioned the actual sales process to be about the numbers. Specifically, we gauged our sales performance by counting how many new leads, how many call-outs, and how many initial tours.

Nineteen months after opening, we found ourselves with over 3,000 qualified prospects, 170 residents, and, most importantly, 50 units still vacant. How could that be? We had at least 60 prospects for every vacancy! The 50 residents we still needed were clearly already in our lead base. "Selling" to those prospects should have been easy, especially with our amazing and innovative community. So why were those 50 units still vacant? That's when I discovered the answer to this puzzle. Hardly any of the higher-functioning prospects were "ready."

I decided that, rather than waiting for these higher-functioning prospects to be forced to move due to a serious health crisis, I would need to figure out some proactive way to help another 50 of them get ready. I wasn't sure how that could be done. Neither was anyone else in our industry. I came to the conclusion that while a transactional, speed-to-lead approach to senior living sales can be effective for those who are forced to move or for the unusual prospect who actually is ready at the time of the inquiry,[2] it is ineffective for the people we most wanted to attract. For the higher-functioning prospects, transactional or value-matching approaches grounded in product- or service-based solutions just doesn't work.

In this book, I will share the lessons learned over the past three decades, pretty much through trial and error, first while in the leasing trenches at The Gatesworth and then at several dozen other hands-on sales turnaround campaigns for third-party operators across the US and Canada.

These turnaround and consulting successes, along with engagements to teach, present, and publish materials that could be used by all industry sales professionals, led to the creation of a theoretical "change" model. My fellow Sherpa co-founder Alexandra (Alex) Fisher and I called our new approach Prospect-Centered Selling (PCS). It is an evidence-based model that we would use to scale our processes through teaching and training others. In the past few years, our core principles have been clarified and confirmed, with extensive sales

---

[2] Having a higher-functioning prospect be "ready" to buy at the time of inquiry was so unusual that we used to affectionately call them "bluebirds." Bluebirds have the motivation to rationally consider features and benefits of your community. Prior to the onslaught of COVID-19 in March of 2020, I have only encountered a handful of higher-functioning IL prospects who didn't start with emotional resistance. The day-to-day isolation and inconveniences of COVID-19, however, seriously impacted older adults living in their own homes—so much so that during the first six months of COVID-19, I personally encountered dozens of IL prospect bluebirds who had become "ready" on their own, even before they inquired.

performance data from Sherpa, a CRM and sales enablement platform created to help sales professionals be more effective.

PCS is a proven, effective approach to senior living sales. It focuses on advancing the prospect's emotional readiness journey instead of trying to sell the benefits of the product. It works by openly and respectfully helping prospects make a buying decision, rather than waiting to process and admit higher-acuity prospects in a crisis. With PCS, sales counselors spend more time with fewer prospects. Higher-functioning prospects need help overcoming emotional resistance.

PCS is a proven, effective approach to senior living sales. It focuses on advancing the prospect's emotional readiness journey, instead of trying to sell the benefits of the product.

That requires a sales counselor to invest the time needed to make an empathic connection, engage in purposeful questioning, and achieve multiple advances. Selling time represents a level of engagement, unlike most other sales performance metrics, which look to the quantity of activity. With PCS, selling time and sales outcomes become qualitative indicators of sales performance.

We developed PCS to significantly grow occupancy and, perhaps more importantly, to give industry sales professionals better tools to help more older adults live better. In the following chapters, we will share what we learned, including:

- Why prospects who are not already in a crisis resist senior living and its typical speed-to-lead sales approach and how to assess, confront, and proactively overcome inherent emotional resistance to moving, one prospect at a time.
- Why the evidence-based theory and processes that comprise PCS help higher-functioning prospects "get ready," improve sales effectiveness, and increase visit-to-move-in conversion rates by as much as 100 percent.

- Why monitoring, tracking, and managing Time in the Selling Zone (TSZ) is a much more relevant and impactful leading indicator and predictor of sales success than reliance on a "more is better" approach focused on generating even more inquiries, call-outs, and/or tours.
- Why investing more of the total selling time available in strategic planning, personalized creative follow-up (CFU), and home visits is key to maximizing your performance.

What follows is a guide to better conversion rates, higher occupancies, upward pressure on rents, and faster fills. Note that PCS sellers close as many need- or crisis-driven prospects as their transactional counterparts. Yet PCS also consistently produces incremental gains from sales to higher-functioning prospects who are generally unresponsive to typical sales tactics. We use theory, data, and prospect case studies to describe and explain why PCS relies on connecting empathically, heroically confronting emotional resistance, and provoking self-persuasion.

PCS is a methodology designed to help prospects "get ready" to buy. It is not about traditional selling, speed-to-lead or volume-and-velocity approaches, which depend on product/service-based solutions. What follows is about the *why* and *what* of PCS, along with a few examples of *how to*.

I invite you to improve your sales effectiveness in senior living or whatever complex sale you are involved with. Together we can transform complex sales professionals to be more effective. For senior living, this translates to filling vacant units, generating value for owners and operators while helping hundreds of thousands more older adults get ready for a new and vibrant chapter in their lives.

Be noble. It's time. Whatever you sell, come join us and become an effective, prospect-centered sales hero!

THE SALES HERO MANIFESTO

I Am A Prospect-Centered Salesperson.

I believe in the life-enhancing opportunities that our product provides.

I am knowledgeable about our product and the industry.

I strive to become knowledgeable about the prospect.

I recognize prospects as people with all of their rich history, complexities, quirks, interests, desires, hopes, and fears. I honor that complexity.

My job is to guide the prospect toward a decision to buy/change.

My job is to build a trusting professional relationship with the prospect.

That relationship is built by planning, by listening, by going to where the prospect is physically and emotionally, and by creatively following up.

My success is measured by my ability to help the prospect go from "I'm not ready" to "I wish I had moved sooner."

My success is measured by my ability to advance the prospect toward a decision to buy/change.

I understand that every prospect is facing a life-changing transition and that ambivalence and resistance are common and real.
I don't give up when I meet resistance or rejection.

I understand that prospects are looking for guidance, trust, and a safe place to voice their motivation, fears, and aspirations for the future.

I understand that prospects don't want to "be sold." Rather, they need help to buy.

I understand that the guidance process requires three steps that I repeat until a decision is made: connecting, untangling, and advancing toward a sale.

I attempt to connect and build a trusting professional relationship with prospects.

I engage in conversations that will help the prospect untangle their emotional resistance to change. I will help the prospect explore the emotional barriers standing in the way of a decision to buy.

I listen with empathy.

I don't interrupt when a prospect is speaking. I maintain eye contact and give visual cues that I am not only hearing what's being said but drinking it in, learning from it, and understanding it. I ask follow-up questions that demonstrate I have listened carefully. I prompt reflection by commenting on the emotional impact of the person's story.

I offer solutions and next steps that are tailored to the prospect's unique journey and their stage of readiness for change. I advance the prospect in taking small steps and building upon those to an eventual decision.

My follow-up with prospects is creative, prompt, and personal. I do this to communicate that the person had an impact on me, I heard what they said, and I am eager to build on a next step.

I "give up the result" and instead focus on my process and behavior. I know that I can't control a prospect's decision, nor can I convince them. Focusing on the pressure to fill units will cause stress and fear for me and place undue pressure on the prospect.

My time is valuable. I spend it where it counts.

I protect and defend my Time in the Selling Zone.

I believe I can help prospects "get ready" when I am able to inspire, facilitate, and assist them in the work of addressing their emotional barriers to change. My success depends on my ability to focus on spending more time with fewer prospects, planning carefully, journaling what I learned, being curious, building trust during tours and home visits, using empathetic listening techniques, and following up creatively.

I AM A SALES HERO!

CHAPTER 1

There Is No Place Like the "Old Folks' Home"

Old age is full of death and full of life. It is a tolerable achievement and it is a disaster. It transcends desire and it taunts it. It is long enough, and it is far from being long enough.

—Ronald Blythe, *The View in Winter*

Senior living communities today aren't your grandmother's version of an *old folks' home*! They are a lot better. Still, the overwhelming majority of today's seniors just "aren't ready" to move anywhere. This chapter addresses the fundamental question: why aren't more qualified prospects following logic and leasing senior living apartments, even when it's in their best interest, and what can we do about it? What if you could help enhance the lives of hundreds of thousands of senior adults by inspiring them to overcome their emotional resistance to moving?

We believe that you can help reluctant prospects "get ready" by adopting a more effective, person-centered approach. An approach that motivates them to leave homes that no longer fit their lifestyle needs. A selling process that embraces clinically proven practices adapted from the psychology of change and is supported by performance data. One that is proven to boost sales, occupancy, and longer-term revenue streams.

A BRIEF HISTORY OF SENIOR LIVING IN THE US

The history of senior housing and care options can help us understand where the outmoded transactional or speed-to-lead selling approach originated in our industry and why it still works in a limited number of settings. However, as the concept of senior living has evolved into a more residential and service-oriented offering that targets higher-functioning prospects, our industry's history also reveals why transactional selling simply doesn't work to convert those higher-functioning prospects who still have choices.

Up until the mid-1960s, congregate living for older people with acute and ongoing healthcare needs ranged from makeshift boarding homes to dedicated group homes run by charitable organizations. They were called by various names: "old folks' homes," "homes for the aged," "boarding homes," "board-and-care homes," "rest homes," and "convalescent homes." Most were operated by a church or the state.

These facilities were typically designed to house fewer than 20 residents and usually had limited funds. They had no licensed nurses. There were minimal service options beyond three meals per day, some housekeeping, and maybe a bus ride to the grocery store or church on Sundays. Beyond attending to personal care needs, none of the services or programs offered anything personalized to the individual residents' preferences. Selling units was not difficult since there were so many more financially challenged seniors who needed the service than there were available rooms.

When the Medicare and Medicaid public aid programs were passed in 1965, many of these homes were converted to licensed skilled nursing facilities (SNFs) with private ownership, oversight, and regulation from state and federal governments. Over time, driven by SNFs and their unlicensed counterparts, the "old folks' home" became more institutional and hospital-like in design, patient relations, and daily operations. These two congregate care options were the only alternatives to staying home or moving in with a family member. Collectively, these are the settings that our current seniors, the silent generation—parents and grandparents of baby boomers—were exposed to when confronting choices for their own aging parents and loved ones.

In those days, crisis-driven seniors themselves had little choice about *whether* or *when* to move to an SNF. They were like hostages that some loved one put into beds at one of these facilities—but only when a calamity of some kind made it impossible for them to continue living on their own. Much like a hospital admission, the placement process for someone moving into an SNF room was entirely transactional. The negative stigma associated with these venues is still in the memory of current-day seniors and generates significant negative, preconceived notions of all congregate senior living options.

In the late 1960s, additional senior living models began to emerge. A number of church groups and other not-for-profit entities began building larger, more residential settings. These developments were motivated by a growing demographic of senior adults, longer lifespans, and a widespread distaste for the institutional nature of existing skilled nursing facilities. These early religious groups and other not-for-profit providers had idealistic values regarding residential environments, service capacity, and a consumer-centered care philosophy. The not-for-profit providers began a paradigm shift in terms of building design, staffing needs, and service offerings. During this early phase, senior housing was financed using two models: life care and refundable entry fee financing. In exchange for giving up a sizable up-front deposit (or in some cases, even all of one's savings) plus a modest monthly fee, residents were either entitled to the return of most of their up-front deposit at termination or, under the life care model, guaranteed housing and care for "the remainder of their lives" and regardless of their future health needs.

With the promise of lifetime care and the backing of the church or another philanthropic sponsor, these communities enjoyed high trust and high occupancies. Again, these early communities filled quickly and without much need to sell. However, unfortunately for their not-for-profit sponsors, the financial model collapsed. With significant advances in healthcare delivery, many people, including senior living residents, began to live well into their eighties and nineties for the first time in history. The volume of senior adults has continued to rise ever since.

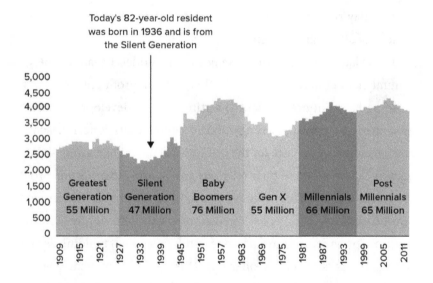

Number of Live Births (1909 to 2013)

Not surprisingly, in their later years, older residents in these communities experienced ever-increasing medical needs. Their ongoing and ever-increasing medical expenses greatly exceeded underwriting expectations. Nearly all of the life care and many of the refundable entry fee communities operating at the time went out of business in the late 1980s.

This includes the original Gatesworth, a well-respected life care community in St. Louis that closed its doors in 1988. It was backed by the Episcopal Presbyterian Church and was known for high standards and excellent service. Unfortunately, The Gatesworth was also trying to operate a life care model that included free long-term healthcare in exchange for what turned out to be an inadequate entry fee. Like all care providers at the time, they were also facing a health cost explosion. The lack of proper underwriting of initial entry fee amounts, combined with the ongoing maintenance needs of an old building in a declining neighborhood, forced them into a financially unstable situation.

In response to the failure of so many of these life care communities across the US, coupled with widespread housing needs, President Ronald Reagan created a sweeping Commission on Housing in 1982. This act made federally insured, mortgage-backed securities underwritten by HUD eligible for private funding sources to develop congregate senior housing communities.

This new generation of retirement communities was modeled around a government-insured but privately funded retirement home. Most of them were offered without large buy-in fees, using a straight rental model. This generation of senior housing was fundamentally different from the "old folks' homes" or SNFs that preceded it. There were three key areas that set these community apart, each designed to make the environment feel more like "home":

- A *residential-style* physical environment both for individual apartment homes and the congregate and community spaces shared by all residents and their guests.
- *Service delivery programs, services, and amenities* provided for both scheduled and on-demand needs, including *optional*

services like housekeeping, personal care, or transportation offered on a fee-for-service basis.

- An *operating philosophy and culture* emphasizing resident choice and control over their own living spaces, schedule of personal routines, and participation in group programs and activities.

These building and operating factors greatly improved the level of resident satisfaction but often did not have the same level of impact on sales conversion results.

HIGH RESIDENT SATISFACTION

Today in the US and Canada, the combination of residential-style facilities, excellent programming and amenities, and the emphasis on resident choice has resulted in very high resident satisfaction at the typical senior living community. According to a study by the American Seniors Housing Association (ASHA) and ProMatura, most residents accept these places as "home" and, moreover, "The overall quality and emotional tone of the lives of residents benefit due to moving into a community."[3]

More specifically, the research found that residents of senior living communities are more likely than their otherwise "matched" stay-at-home counterparts to:

- Be happy with their daily lives.
- Spend more time connecting and engaging with people and less time watching TV.
- Say that their health is better today than it was two years ago.

---

[3] ProMatura Match Study for ASHA (2006), *Prospective Independent Living Customers—Key Study of Prospects and Hold Outs.*

The ASHA/ProMatura resident satisfaction study found that resident (or customer) satisfaction reported across various congregate home settings, financial models, level of care, and geographies was very high. Compared to industry reporting, seniors moving into senior residences rated higher in customer satisfaction than customers at luxury resorts, hotels, or cruise ships.

Even during the 2020 COVID-19 pandemic, when senior living communities faced enormous hardships, a majority of senior living residents and their family members praised management and staff for the safety and comfort they got during the initial wave of COVID-19 shutdowns.[4] Furthermore, four to six weeks after moving into a senior living community, nearly every higher-functioning resident before and during COVID-19 told me in one form or another, "I wish I had moved here sooner."

Like other senior living residents, these new customers are likely to give their new home within a senior community high marks for giving them:

- Control over whether to spend the day in their apartment or engage socially in one of many recreational, educational, and fitness programs or other activities.
- Choices for meals, fitness, activities, and transportation.
- Access to personal care or medication oversight, if needed.
- A sense of security, safety, and peace of mind for the residents and their families.

---

[4] Based on results from 2,000 resident surveys taken by Activated Insights and reported in *Senior Housing News*. Sudo, Chuck. "Covid-19 'Caution Fatigue' Taking Hold, But Most Senior Living Residents Satisfied." *Senior Housing News*, 13 July 2020, https://seniorhousingnews.com/2020/07/13/covid-19-caution-fatigue-taking-hold-but-most-senior-living-residents-satisfied/.

THE GATESWORTH:
FILLING A LUXURY SENIOR LIVING COMMUNITY

The potential to help older people enjoy these very benefits transformed my life. In 1988, with hopes of building my own senior living campus, I left behind 10 years of practicing law, a large client base, and significant income, all in the hopes of finding a career that was more heroic than representing clients who were usually fighting over money. Setting out with a few like-minded partners to help older adults find a more fulfilling lifestyle seemed like a good choice. Located in my hometown of St. Louis, The Gatesworth was purpose-built as an upscale IL community.

We faced an uphill battle. At the time, there was nothing like The Gatesworth in St. Louis, and there were only a handful of comparable models anywhere in the US. We were going to develop an essentially unknown product for an aging population that was instinctively resistant to change. On top of this, the rental fees were considerably higher than what multifamily apartment complexes with comparably sized apartments were charging. A number of potential lending sources thought we were nuts.

Promotional photos for The Gatesworth, including
resident services and exterior

David signs an early Gatesworth prospect

Like a lot of first-time developers, I primarily focused on generating as many new inquiries and qualified leads as possible. Over the years, however, I found that it's relatively easy to build an adequate lead base in senior housing. That's because our total industry penetration of qualified prospects is so low. Only around 10 percent of age- and income-qualified prospects, people who would benefit from their programs and amenities, ever move into senior living com-

Without any existing communities to compare with or learn from, we mostly just made things up, such as the unit floor plans, pricing, number, size, and configuration of common spaces, amenities, programs, and services. Our intention was to create an environment not for "old folks" but rather a community that we ourselves, then in our mid30s, would want to live in. It was a community where our mantra became "the answer is yes" to any request relating to our programs, experiences, or service offerings. Perhaps the best thing we had going for ourselves is that we didn't have any idea of how hard it was going to be!

munities. Generating an inquiry from only a small portion of the remaining 90 percent is relatively easy. Nearly every community can succeed at generating enough inquiries.

It was nearly two years into our marketing program for The Gatesworth when I had my first major aha moment. I looked at our total number of active leads per vacant unit. Imagine my shock when I discovered that I had 3,000 active leads and 50 empty units—a ratio of 60:1! This ratio became a go-to metric to see if a community actually needed more leads. For the first time, I realized that if we were able to convert even a small percentage of our 3,000-prospect lead base, then the 50 additional residents we needed to find were already there. They just weren't *ready* yet.

Rather than waiting for new, urgent inquiries or for existing prospects to suffer a terrible health crisis, I would need to find some other more proactive way to help another 50 prospects get ready to buy. I wasn't sure whether or how that could be done. And, at the time, neither was anyone else in our industry.

Let me illustrate the challenge by introducing you to Mitch, one of the higher-functioning prospects who just wasn't ready.

CASE STUDY: MY EXPERIENCE WITH MITCH

When we met, Mitch was a spunky 90-year-old. He was very sociable, enjoyed a good game of gin rummy, and loved to tell stories, usually about his World War II experiences. His little black poodle, Molly, was usually at his side. Suffering from emphysema, Mitch sometimes struggled with shortness of breath. He drove a 10-year-old red Ford pickup with a built-in hoist to transport a wheelchair, just in case.

After the death of his wife, Mitch moved from the farm to the city to live with his daughter Ellen. Before moving in, Mitch had paid off Ellen's mortgage and built, at his own expense, a new first-floor bedroom suite. Per Mitch, he moved there, heroically, "to help Ellen." Just before Mitch moved, Ellen, at age 50, had gotten married. She and her new husband worked for an international charitable organization. The two of them traveled frequently, leaving Mitch alone most days. He usually dined solo while watching TV.

Mitch became isolated and bored. He had been diagnosed with early-onset Alzheimer's and suffered from pulmonary disease and acute arthritis. He was on a complicated medication regimen and used very small handwritten notes, jotted with a short wooden pencil in a small spiral-bound notepad, to remind himself when to take his medications and breathing treatments. It didn't appear to be a very reliable system, even to Mitch. Ellen and her husband were feeling a little guilty about not being able to spend more time with Mitch. They were seriously concerned about his health and his ability to continue living mostly on his own, so they called our community.

We talked on the phone several times, and Mitch gave me permission to visit him at Ellen's home. Ellen and her husband were encouraging him to move sooner rather than later.

Mitch told me that he understood his daughter's concerns, but he was certainly not ready to move anywhere. He said that he couldn't afford it, even though we already had discussed that he was qualified for a significant VA Aid and Attendance pension that would cover most of his rent. When he expressed concerns about Ellen's well-being and his need to live with her, Ellen assured him that she was now happily married and well provided for. By the time we left, it was clear to Ellen and to me that, logically, Mitch's well-being, socialization, and quality of life would be enhanced by a move. Just compare:

Status Quo	Advantages of Moving
1. Isolated and unnoticed	1. Companionship and people to listen to and admire him
2. Dependent on daughter	2. Realign relationship with daughter
3. Depressed and stuck	3. Confidence from a fresh start
4. Can't manage meds but waiting "until I can't reach the freezer"	4. Assistance when needed and increased independence
5. Care costs increasing	5. With VA benefits, costs less per month and all-inclusive pricing

> But Mitch wasn't operating logically. "Whenever I do become ready, I will definitely move to your place," he told me. The where of his move was settled. When asked when he thought he might be ready, Mitch just laughed. He intended to stay put for "as long as possible." Always a bit of a jokester, Mitch thought a little further. He then lifted his arthritic arm toward the refrigerator and said, "I'll be ready to move when I can't reach the freezer to get my ice cream anymore!" From a transactional perspective, Mitch had no urgency and just went "cold."

Like most senior living sales professionals at the time, I authentically wanted to help Mitch improve his situation. But I was failing miserably. His resistance was rooted in the negative experiences his family members had had at an institutional nursing home and, ever the hero, his proud sense of self-determination. I had no experience, theoretical model, engagement tools, or strategic plan to help him confront or overcome his deeply emotional resistance.

I had no experience, no theoretical model, no engagement tools, or any strategic plan to help him confront or overcome his deeply emotional resistance.

From my transactional perspective, there were several times along the way that I thought we had already "closed" Mitch on signing a lease and moving in. After our second tour, we created a favorable pricing offer and were very confident. We sent him home with a lease plus one of his favorite desserts and a handwritten thank-you note. But the day after evaluating our offering and hearing all the logical arguments we could come up with for him to move, Mitch just said, "No, I'm not ready yet." He went from a hot to a cold lead with those few words. We were frustrated and discouraged by the fierce and ongoing rejection from Mitch.

We knew prospects like Mitch were the people for whom we designed our communities. But when it came to converting these prospects into residents, we were failing miserably. Today, over 30 years later, many senior living providers are still struggling. On average, in 2020, in a typical IL rental community, less than 10 percent of those who inquired and only about 20 percent of prospects who actually toured (tour to move-in ratio) ever signed a lease and moved in.

Given the enormous benefits as well as the high level of satisfaction among existing residents at each of these levels of care, it just doesn't make sense logically that so few higher-functioning prospects who inquired and invested the time to tour actually moved in. Determined to figure out how to help Mitch "get ready," we began to study the sources of prospect readiness and some techniques to help prospects confront deep-seated emotional resistance.

CHAPTER 2

Confronting Emotional Resistance, One Prospect at a Time

Older adults see where they live as the Alamo and will make their last stand defending it. We try to advance with logic, manipulations, and threats, and they use any means at their disposal to repel us... They know that once they lose what they call home, the "endgame" begins, and there's no going back.

—David Solie[5]

L ogic and reason would suggest that not only Mitch but nearly every qualified prospect who seeks information about one of our communities would benefit from moving. But I found that virtually every older adult was so emotionally resistant to moving anywhere that very few of them would even call to inquire. Before we could help these prospects confront and hopefully overcome their resistance, we needed to understand more about its sources.

---

[5] www.facebook.com/agingparentcoach. "Home Rules: We're Not Going Anywhere." *Aging, Caregiving and the Journey through the Second Half of Life*, 21 May 2020, www.davidsolie.com/blog/home-rules-were-not-going-anywhere /.

OVERRELIANCE ON A
SPEED-TO-LEAD SALES APPROACH

When I first began selling at The Gatesworth, like most industry professionals, I thought of the sales process as transactional, driven by logical benefits. I assumed that demand for a better lifestyle would be strong, with lots of interest. Accordingly, and mistakenly, I adopted a sales approach designed to capture that demand quickly. The sales approach was known as "volume and velocity" or "speed to lead." To me, selling this new, residential, service-enriched product was going to be much like filling a skilled nursing bed or selling a single-family home, only easier. I thought that I would present one-size-fits-all, product-oriented options. I thought that they were deciding, actually choosing among available product choices. In this context, my sales approach was touting features like exciting floor plans, large closets, granite countertops, beautiful views, community dining, entertainment venues, fitness centers, manicured grounds, and so on. Like a traditional sale, I anticipated and prepared to overcome objections and then close. This approach worked, but not with the prospects to whom I wanted to sell.

Like a traditional sale, I anticipated and prepared to overcome objections and then close. This approach worked, but not with the prospects to whom I wanted to sell.

In the world of senior living, a speed-to-lead approach can be effective in specific situations where urgency and velocity are inherent. For example:

- When the prospect is forced to move somewhere, *anywhere*, and is thereby forced to be "ready" to decide.
- With professional referral sources for need-driven prospects, as these interactions are closer to demand-driven or business-to-business sales.

- With some higher-acuity offerings like short-term rehabilitation and later-stage memory care.[6]

In situations where, due to a crisis, the prospect is necessarily going to move somewhere the faster you respond (the *velocity* part of the volume-and-velocity methodology), the more likely they will be to choose your place rather than that of a competitor.

The critical decision-making issue for someone referred to or "being placed" into a skilled nursing home in this model is not *whether* to move or even *when*. Rather, it is simply about *where*. The admissions staff at nursing homes learns what they need to know from medical records payor sources and standardized forms and then communicates or sells favorable facility features. SNFs are selling the senior living's ultimate "show and tell."

Little or no time is spent building trusting relationships, getting to know the person's feelings or life story, planning next steps, doing home visits, or following up to nurture prospects. Instead, necessity and the rapid pace of ongoing resident turnover dictate that the highest priority goes to the frailest, most urgent, need-driven prospects. The sales cycle, if one can really call it that, is very short, and as you might expect, conversion rates for skilled nursing prospects are high. The process usually takes days, sometimes even hours. Definitely not weeks or months.

Unfortunately, in practice, when you use the speed-to-lead, skilled nursing approach in higher-functioning settings like IL, AL, memory care (MC), or continuing care retirement communities (CCRCs), a singular focus on converting prospects who are ready washes out most of the very nonurgent prospects, like Mitch, who you built the

---

[6] "Since these types of higher-acuity offerings tend to be more standardized and more demand-driven, there is less need to personalize the sales activity." Homburg, Christian, et al. "When Should the Customer Really Be King? On the Optimum Level of Salesperson Customer Orientation in Sales Encounters." *Journal of Marketing*, vol. 75, no. 2, 2011, pp. 55–74., doi:10.1509/jmkg.75.2.55.

community for. That's how I wound up at The Gatesworth with 60 active leads for every vacant unit. I was treating Mitch and his thousands of peers as "cold," unclosable prospects. Collectively and individually, I gave up on them.

It's true that focusing on prospects who are already in crisis, the need-driven prospects, makes a one-size-fits-all selling process easier for senior living communities. But it also makes operating and attracting new, more vibrant prospects later more difficult.

It's true that focusing on prospects who are already in crisis, the need-driven prospects, makes a one-size-fits-all selling process easier for senior living communities. But it also makes operating and attracting new, more vibrant prospects later more difficult. As crisis-driven prospects move into more residential, service-enriched living environments, they create a number of unwanted consequences. High-urgency prospects typically are the least desirable customers, in part because they have the shortest stays. Their care needs put administrative, service, and care resource strains on the operations staff. Moreover, accepting more need-driven residents makes it even harder to attract other healthier, more discretionary prospects like Mitch to senior living communities in the future.

In terms of the sales conversion process, the speed-to-lead selling process focuses on:

1. Identifying a prospect's unmet needs in their current situation, usually physical, health, or behavioral limitations. For Mitch, these are the logical reasons he should move.
2. Matching these needs to the community's features and benefits in an effort to close the sale (benefits or value matching) as quickly as possible.

When they think about sales, a large majority of today's senior living owners, investors, and operational leaders still resort to transactional selling. This includes its nomenclature, metrics, and weak conversion rates. Typically, their working sales strategy is tied to the speed-to-lead approach. Their mantra is, "More leads, more call-outs, more tours."

Speed-to-lead sellers classify prospects based on their sales pipeline phases: initial contact, pre-tour, post-tour, and move-in-process. Prospects are assumed to proceed in a linear progression from initial inquiry to move-in. Each lead is also classified as "hot," "warm," or "cold" based on their perceived sense of urgency. Sales efforts are focused on performing a small number of specific engagement tasks (call-outs, email-outs, and tours), preferably with the newest leads and other hot prospects. The objective of these tasks is to use logic, value matching, and persuasion to close as many prospects as possible as soon as possible. Those who don't close after a couple of call-outs and a tour, like Mitch, are reclassified either as "cold" or "future" leads.

The overall sales strategy and tactics are simple: close first on touring the community and then on making a deposit. During face-to-face and voice-to-voice engagements, a transactional sales professional may rely on multiple attempts to convince, persuade, and close. They think, "Get to yes or no as quickly as possible. If yes, close. If no, put into a cold stack, save for later, and move on to the next inquiry." When all else fails, transactional sellers often turn to a real estate selling style, with takeaways and discounts.

These sales behaviors do not take into account the customer's personal emotional decision-making journey. They are instead driven by gross revenue projections that investors expect based on the budgeted pro forma revenue needed to reach positive net operating income (NOI). After all, key investor metrics and underlying sales strategies are typically pro forma rather than prospect-focused and centered.

I know this because as an owner and operator, I formulated sales strategies designed to meet investor pro forma projections. That was my starting point when we opened The Gatesworth. I was laser-focused on what we needed to get to meet pro forma occupancy numbers. The customer's emotional resistance never appeared on our radar. If a product- or solution-oriented approach had worked early on, I would probably still be using it. But it didn't work.

THE CHALLENGE: INSPIRING A DESIRE TO BUY

As I struggled to identify an alternative to transactional selling, I began to consider whether and how sales counselors could confront the prospect's emotional resistance by inspiring and increasing their motivation or desire to buy.

The idea that a desire to buy is an indispensable ingredient needed for closing is well supported by sales gurus like Brian Tracy. Tracy is a well-respected sales thought leader and author of *The Psychology of Selling*.[7] Early on in our search for an effective senior living sales methodology, we relied heavily on Tracy's theory. He defined a "sale" as what happens when there is a "transfer of enthusiasm and confidence" from the seller to the buyer. He identifies four prerequisites that must be met prior to closing any kind of sale, no matter the nature of the goods or services. We agree. They are:

- The customer must be *able to afford* the product or service.
- They must be *able to use it* (in senior living, this generally relates to their health qualifications).
- They must *need it* (none of this generation of senior living prospects would inquire unless they had a clear and present need).
- They must *want or have a desire for it.*

---

[7] Tracey, B. *The Psychology of Selling: The Art of Closing Sales.* audiobook ed., Nightingale-Conant Corp., 1995.

From my home sales experience, I knew how to quickly and efficiently qualify and discover whether any or all of Tracy's closing prerequisites were present in any potential home buyer. They were part of my initial prospect qualifying and discovery process. Once a real estate salesperson believes that a prospective buyer meets Tracy's four closing prerequisites, they then move on to identifying unfulfilled needs that are then matched to specific features and benefits of any house under consideration. The real estate selling style tends to be reactive, pre-programmed, mechanical, and one-size-fits-all. This methodology will appropriately value, count, and reward more leads, more call-outs, and more tours. Since there is ongoing demand, it also determines whether the potential home buyer is likely to close as quickly as possible. And if not, it dictates that you move on to the next prospect.

That is exactly the sales scenario I knew and the one that I was expecting during my first attempts to fill The Gatesworth. It is also the paradigm that most senior living owner-operators still use today to gauge and predict sales velocity as well as to evaluate and reward sales performance. However, in practice, I soon found that a transactional approach works a lot better in home sales than in senior living sales.

Senior living sales counselors, like their real estate and skilled nursing counterparts, can screen new inquiries from higher-functioning prospects to be sure that they are financially qualified (in Tracy's words, whether *they can afford* to live there). Senior living prospects also can be health-qualified for the level of care offered at a community. This means that in Tracy's paradigm, we can discover whether or not prospects *can use it*. As for Tracy's third criterion, *they must need it*. Mitch and nearly every senior living prospect who reaches out to inquire *needs to move,* even though they strongly resist efforts to close.

The challenge is that in practice, only about 10 percent of otherwise qualified senior living prospects *want or have a desire for it*. And that

10 percent is typically made up of prospects with an urgency driven by a health-related crisis. In terms of desire, crisis-driven senior living prospects are a lot more like home buyers or skilled nursing candidates than their higher-functioning counterparts.

The remaining 90 percent of our senior living prospects not only lack the desire to move, but they also perceive moving from home as something to avoid or certainly postpone. At best, moving is almost always a "plan B" option. In this context, the buying and decision-making process is out of sync with a transactional selling process. For these higher-functioning prospects, making a decision to move any-where is a highly emotional, nonlinear, very personal, and primarily irrational process.

In reality, senior living sales counselors are asking prospects to consider a sea change. We are asking people like Mitch to redefine them-selves, leave their current role identities behind, and start writing one of the last chapters in their life. We are not just selling Mitch a new apartment with communal facilities and on-site services and care. What we are really trying to sell him is a life change. It's not a small change but a fundamental redefinition of the self. It's a change in his desire to provide for his family, his fatherly identity. It's a change that provokes a profound re-contextualization of his role, his purpose, and his relationship with family and the outside world. Beneath the façade of choosing an apartment, this is a complex and emotionally charged proposition.

We are not just selling Mitch a new apartment with communal facilities and on-site services and care. What we are really trying to sell him is a life change. It's not a small change but a fundamental redefinition of the self.

The key to more effective sales results with any complex, emotion-laden sale lies in how we overcome this critical prerequisite by realigning with the buyer's emotional decision-making process. Successful conversion of more higher-functioning senior living prospects has to do with confronting and untangling emotional resistance to buying before trying to sell solutions.

SOURCES OF EMOTIONAL RESISTANCE TO SENIOR LIVING

The key to more effective sales results with any complex, emotion-laden sale lies in how we overcome this critical prerequisite by realigning with the buyer's emotional decision-making process. Successful conversion of more higher-functioning senior living prospects has to do with confronting and untangling emotional resistance to buying before trying to sell solutions.

When asked, very few people, and even fewer prospects, will tell you directly what's going on emotionally. Most, like Mitch, rarely share negative preconceptions or fears related to old stories, even after they have good reason to trust your intentions. When we ask what prompted them to call us, they often hide behind something like, "I'm just calling to check out my options." But this response is no more likely to be accurate than it would be for someone calling to "check out options" with a brain surgeon or divorce attorney. It just doesn't happen, especially not when older adults call for themselves.

Many senior living sales counselors, particularly those who use a transactional style, aren't prepared to seek out, understand, or address emotional resistance. They aren't in the mindset, nor are they equipped to handle the personal emotional investment or the amount of sales time needed to "get personal." Instead, they have either adopted or by default are using an efficient, time-saving, and mostly ineffective order-taking approach to new inquiries.

When they perceive a lack of prospect urgency from Mitch and other higher-functioning prospects, they assume a lack of interest. They classify the prospect as "cold" and look for new, more urgent leads. The solution and challenge for senior living communities is to create a sales approach and a sales culture that will enable them to attract, convert, and fill with higher-functioning, rather than higher-acuity, prospects. People like Mitch. People who have strong underlying emotional resistance.

Moving from a family home into an age-segregated community for higher-functioning prospects like Mitch forces them to give up a sense of their core identity, their nostalgic sense of familiarity, comfort, and security. Each individual has their own unique version of what makes up their personal legacy and sense of "home." For Mitch, his core identity was strongly associated with his role vis-à-vis his family as a provider, protector, and self-reliant, wartime hero figure. As such, his natural resistance to changing these life-defining roles was amplified when it was associated with the idea of moving into a senior living community. This amplification is generally caused by a combination of factors: generational, cultural, and developmental bias.

Each individual has their own unique version of what makes up their personal legacy and sense of "home."

A. Generational Bias

Most often, this silent generation of older adults, as well as their baby boomer children, have a very negative perception of age-segregated, congregate housing. They see it as a last resort. Their overall strategy for dealing with aging is to deny, deflect, and, whenever possible, postpone making any changes, and certainly not to call to explore different living options.

This is the generation who brought their aging parents (and/or grandparents) into their own homes with multiple generations of family members under one roof. Hardly anyone from their generation would even consider sending someone to "one of those places." In their parents' day, to get someone to move, you would have to physically take them.

Families would only put someone into an "old folks' home" or an SNF in situations that were perceived to be dishonorable or shameful—for example, situations where the older person was:

- Too sick for the family to care for. They would be so sick that, however dishonorable, the family could justify casting them out for their own good.
- Mentally impaired. The silent generation saw shame in mental illness and considered those afflicted as a source of disgrace.
- Very poor. Indigent families couldn't support an aging senior within the household. This left no reasonable choice but to put them into an old folks' home, despite the shame.
- From ungrateful and uncaring families or without any loved ones at all. Again, this was seen as shameful behavior.

When we met, Mitch had recently sold his family's farm after the death of his wife. He had also lost a daughter to breast cancer and a son to diabetes. Each of them had spent their last days and years suffering in an institutional skilled nursing setting. For Mitch, these end-of-life experiences of his family members created a significant negative perception of all senior living communities. It brought tears to his eyes whenever he spoke about their horrific situations in what he referred to as the "warehouses of death." Mitch was determined to avoid ever moving "to one of those places."

This negative preconceived attitude is common among the silent generation. So when one of his peers calls and asks about senior living, it is first and foremost a signal that something very problematic and maybe even shameful is already going on. Logic be damned. Negative preconceived notions arise in the form of objections and resistance to even considering a more supportive environment. Research confirms that "older adults fear the loss of independence and senior housing more than death. When asked what they fear most, seniors rated loss of independence (26%) and moving out of home into a nursing home (13%) as their greatest fears. Just 3% of seniors indicated that death was their greatest fear."[8] Consequentially, the early stages of the customer's "whether to move" decision-making process are emotional, not factual. The emotions result from fear and resistance to any lifestyle change, but especially a significant and critical one like a move to senior living.

B. Cultural Ageist Bias

Moving to a senior living community naturally identifies someone as "old!" For Mitch and others like him, inherent resistance to change is further amplified by a negative cultural bias against "old age" in our society.

"Everyday ageism is part of American culture and one of the most common and socially condoned forms of prejudice and discrimination."

"Everyday ageism is part of American culture and one of the most common and socially condoned forms of prejudice and discrimination."[9] More than 80 percent of older Americans commonly experience at least one form of ageism each day. Over one-third have internalized stereotypes to the degree that they "agreed" or "strongly agreed" that loneliness or depression are inherent parts of aging.[10]

These perceptions and ageist experiences run directly counter to Mitch's values of self-reliance and his role as a provider and protector of Ellen, his only remaining family member. Against this backdrop, the very thought of moving into "one of those old folks' homes" adds to his resistance to moving.

---

[8] "Aging in Place in America" study commissioned by Clarity® and The EAR Foundation. https://www.marketingcharts.com/demographics-and-audiences/boomers-and-older-2343.

[9] Futurity, https://www.futurity.org/ageism-older-adults-survey-2402802/

[10] The University of Michigan Institute for Healthcare Policy and Innovation's National Poll on Healthy Aging (https://www.healthyagingpoll.org/report/everyday-ageism-and-health).

C. Developmental Bias

What further builds onto this mix of negative perceptions that Mitch and others have about senior living is a change-resistant, personal "developmental agenda." David Solie, an expert in geriatric psychology, contends that the older adults' developmental agenda places a strong premium on preserving the status quo (especially one's housing) in order to maintain whatever control each older adult has left.[11]

Even as higher-functioning prospects like Mitch experience frustration and dissatisfaction about living alone and have wavering confidence in their continued ability to perform necessary self-care or medication management, they continue to resist moving, usually until some serious health or other crisis forces them to do so.

OLDER ADULT BUYING DECISION CHARACTERISTICS

- "Older adults do not process information at the same rate as they did when they were younger. We assume this means that they have slowed down in all areas of mental functioning. The assumption is wrong. Modern research has shown that while processing time is slowed while we age, information management skills, reasoning skills, IQ, verbal ability, and vocabulary are all preserved."[12]
- Congregate or age-segregated housing reminds this generation of the old folks' home of their youth and evokes negative preconceived emotional resistance.

---

[11] Solie, D. (2004). How to Say It to Seniors: Closing the Communication Gap with Our Elders. New York: Penguin, p. 17.

[12] David Solie, The 7 Common Mistakes Professionals Make Communicating with Seniors, 2004 (p. 17). More on David Solie in [Chapter 5]

- Personalized attention is expected and appreciated. They expect sales counselors to go out of their way to accommodate. That is what professionals like doctors, lawyers, insurance agents, and others did when they were young adults.
- Today's seniors are less likely to change residence than any other age group. Only about 5 percent of people over 75 change their residence in any given year.
- The perception of ongoing financial security is critical due to Depression-era experiences. Regardless of how much they have, they are forever concerned with the possibility of running out of money. Moreover, many consider "spending on themselves" to be self-indulgent and quite unnatural.

If they were ever to move to a community, they are most attracted to a place that "feels like home."

A SALES METHODOLOGY DESIGNED TO CONFRONT EMOTIONAL RESISTANCE

A direct consequence of this strong emotional resistance to leaving "home" is that converting higher-functioning prospects to residents is both complex and difficult. These individuals require personalized, strategic planning and a lot of selling time to address layers of deep-seated emotional resistance. Selling product benefits or solutions to higher-functioning prospects too soon, before they've had time to become aware of and then confront these issues, can slow or shut down the entire decision-making process.

What would have helped Mitch and other prospects (not to mention our fledgling development company) was a more effective sales methodology. It needed to be field-tested, supported by evidence-based theory and relevant sales metrics. We were still using three-by-five index cards and Excel spreadsheets to track activities. So an effective methodology would preferably be supported by a purpose-built CRM that could gauge progress and help plan next steps. The methodology and the data would help leasing counselors, as well as those who oversee their efforts, assess and decide how to invest available sales hours, predict results, plan meaningful next steps, and deliver data to improve the team's sales performance. During the initial fill of The Gatesworth, I was under a lot of pressure to create and execute a better sales model as soon as possible.

From my current vantage point today, 30-plus years later, I can say with certainty that the occupancy challenge we faced during our initial fill of The Gatesworth in 1988 wasn't based on any factors like location, building layout, programs, amenities, staff, insufficient number of qualified leads, or even pricing.[13] Rather, the challenge was our steadfast reliance on an ineffective sales methodology.

Rather, the challenge was our steadfast reliance on an ineffective sales methodology.

A. What is Prospect-Centered Selling?

There is an approach proven to be more effective at increasing sales conversions in senior living. Per David Solie, "Professionals who try to drive older clients with artificial deadlines and high-pressure closing

---

[13] This is true more than ever during the COVID-19 pandemic. It has caused all of us feel the sense of isolation, inconvenience, and uncertainty that many senior adults feel every day. Logically, the argument to move into a protected, service-enriched senior living community is stronger than ever. Still, while the first six months of the pandemic saw new inquiries initially fall and then return to pre-COVID-19 levels, prospect conversion rates from visit to move-in have remained about the same. For further details, see the *Sherpa Sales Performance Data Report*, https://sherpacrm.com/2020/07/10/from-the-data-team-july covid-19-sales-performance-report/

Professionals who try to drive older clients with artificial deadlines and high-pressure closing techniques usually find out they don't work. Focus on the quality of your connection (using stories and metaphors). They will signal when they are ready to move forward.

techniques usually find out they don't work. Focus on the quality of your connection (using stories and metaphors). They will signal when they are ready to move forward." [14] Taking Solie's advice to heart, my Sherpa co-founder Alex Fisher and I developed a one-on-one PCS style with sales strategies, metrics, and approaches that are customer-centered rather than built around the product or investors. [15] The intention and the results have been to elevate sales and achieve:

- Faster fills
- Higher occupancies
- Reduced need for lead generation
- Higher-functioning residents
- Less discounting
- More fun and reduced turnover for the sales team

A side-by-side comparison of transactional selling and PCS highlights the key differences between the two styles:

---

[14] Solie, David. *How to Say It to Seniors Closing the Communication Gap with Our Elders.* Prentice Hall Press, 2004.

[15] Smith, David, and Alexandra Fisher. "Measuring Success in Seniors Housing Sales: Prospect-Centered Selling® with the 'Stages of Change' Model." *Seniors Housing & Care Journal*, 2012, p. 32. .

Table 1. Comparing Transactional with Prospect-Centered Selling.

	Transactional Selling	Prospect-Centered Selling
Focus	Product features and benefits	Prospect's stage of readiness for change
Vital Behaviors	Uncover prospect's product needs and then value match with product offerings. Communicate what is different and better compared to competitive offerings. Generate as many new inquiries as possible. Give priority to new inquiries and minimize time with any particular prospect. Persuade and convince.	Assess prospect's stage of readiness and then engage in ongoing planning and personalized creative follow-up. Build trusting relationships, explore life stories, and uncover and address underlying emotional resistance, especially with prospects in denial and thinking stages. Motivate self-awareness and a desire for change, especially for prospects in denial and thinking stages. Shift to a more transactional style for prospects in planning and action stages.
Pipeline Milestones	Inquiry Initial tour Deposit Move-in Perceived sense of urgency	Inquiry Initial tour Stage of readiness: denial, thinking, planning, or action Advances along continuum of change Deposit Move-in

Outcomes Thought to Favorably Impact Conversion Ratios	Number of sales activities (call-outs, follow-up mailers, event invites, and tours)	Number of prospect advances
		Time in the Selling Zone
		Strategic plans for next prospect interaction
	Number of total leads generated	
	Number of prospects who have a high level of urgency to move anywhere	

Unlike a transactional approach, PCS doesn't assume the prospect is ready to buy, meaning to give up their home in exchange for a better lifestyle. It acknowledges and addresses negative emotional resistance based on generational, cultural, developmental, and personal emotional factors. It is characterized by a purposeful and personalized sales strategy to build readiness to create a new "home" in each prospect, one at a time.

PCS was designed to help individual prospects confront and embrace their emotional resistance to moving, even if a move may be necessary to enhance their quality of life. The intention is for the sales counselor to align with the prospect in a nonjudgmental way. Counselors succeed when they concentrate on building trust, discover what their prospects value, and assess the extent to which they are ready to change.

Rather than trying to convince or persuade, PCS engages the prospect in a manner that is collaborative, evocative, and reflective.

Rather than trying to convince or persuade, PCS engages the prospect in a manner that is collaborative, evocative, and reflective. Our strategic approach to selling senior housing combines the science of multi-call sales from Neil Rackham's SPIN Selling[16]

---

[16] Rackham, N. (1988). *SPIN Selling.* New York: McGraw-Hill.

with a transtheoretical model adapted from the "psychology of readiness for change."[17]

For sales counselors dealing with prospects like Mitch, PCS is based on selling a willingness to accept change before offering product-based solutions. The psychology of change first addresses the customer's emotional barriers to change and ultimately their desire to buy. The science addresses the sales team's need to make strategic advances over multiple interactions to help reluctant prospects get ready for a difficult life transition. All of this takes time.

The science addresses the sales team's need to make strategic advances, over multiple interactions, to help reluctant prospects get ready for a difficult life transition. All of this takes time.

B. The Three-Phase Senior Living Selling Process

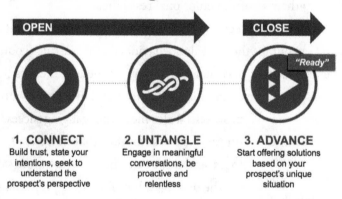

Senior Living Sales Process

1. CONNECT	2. UNTANGLE	3. ADVANCE
Build trust, state your intentions, seek to understand the prospect's perspective	Engage in meaningful conversations, be proactive and relentless	Start offering solutions based on your prospect's unique situation

PCS is based on a three-phase sales process with milestones oriented to the sales counselor's progress. Each of these phases invites specific strategies to facilitate change, promote readiness to buy, and convert prospects:

---

[17] Prochaska, J. O., Norcross, J. C., & DiClemente, C. C. (1995), *Changing for Good.* New York: Harper.

1. **Connecting** through empathic, trust-building interactions with a prospect, whether voice to voice, face to face, through the mail, or electronically.

2. **Untangling** emotional resistance to help the prospect become aware and then, hopefully, motivated to reframe even considering a move.

3. **Advancing** by getting a prospect commitment, however small, that moves the prospect closer to being ready to buy.

Sales counselors will need to employ and then repeat these principles with prospects like Mitch multiple times. This might happen during initial conversations, home visits, tours, or other interactions. When sales counselors shift their focus away from the product or solutions early on, they can learn a lot. They discover who their prospects really are, who they were, what they value, what motivates them, and what might help them confront emotional resistance.

As an executive director (ED) or sales manager, you will want to support and encourage the key sales behaviors that make sales counselors more effective. That may mean giving up antiquated metrics that are intended to limit the counselor's ability to spend more time with fewer prospects. It also means not gauging success based on the false assumption that more leads, more tours, and more call-outs generate more sales.

It also means not gauging success based on the false assumption that more leads, more tours, and more call-outs generate more sales.

The demographics for age-appropriate senior housing prospects are growing. The product and service options are even more attractive. But without some help to overcome deep-seated emotional resistance, very few prospects voluntarily choose senior living. In large part, that is because the most widely used sales strategy is still tied to a transactional, speed-to-lead approach.

This antiquated model is still considered by large segments of our industry—especially its investors, lenders, and operators—to be the "emperor" of senior living sales. As I learned in the selling trenches while filling The Gatesworth and again leading dozens of turnaround fill campaigns under the consulting

The speed-to-lead approach is like an emperor—who has no clothes!

banner of One On One and the sales enablement platform Sherpa, we can do better. The speed-to-lead approach is like an emperor—who has no clothes!

CHAPTER 3

Vital Behaviors
That Drive Conversions

In baseball, a hitter should be measured by his success in that which
he is trying to do which is to create runs...Because that was not
obvious, at least to the people who ran baseball, [Billy Beane and the
Oakland A's] smelled a huge opportunity.

—Michael Lewis, *Moneyball*

Back in 1988, I was very confident when I told my partners, Charlie, Bob, and Elana, "If you figure out how to build The Gatesworth, I'll figure out how to fill it." I had a plan to enhance the commonly used transactional SNF sales process. My intention was to draw on three sources: my own successful experience with real estate sales, my study of senior living industry thought leaders,[18] and my research of techniques used by nationally recognized sales figures outside of senior living, including Zig Ziglar, Brian Tracy, James Cathcart, and Tom Hopkins. But to my chagrin, the selling skills and approaches I learned from real estate sales and from studying traditional sales theory didn't work very well when it came to converting senior living prospects.

During the initial fill of The Gatesworth, it didn't take long for me to figure out that I needed to develop a more effective sales methodology.

---

[18] Including, Joe Newland, Jim Moore, Linda Todd, Margaret Wylde, Barbra Kleger, and Tony Mullen.

If I was not successful, the results would be disastrous. It would destroy my reputation and force bankruptcy not only for me but for my partners, friends, and family as well.

My own sink-or-swim financial situation was highly motivating, as I personally ran out of money 15 months after opening and had to scramble for cash to meet living expenses. Through a lot of trial and error, I eventually figured out how to convert enough prospects to fill every one of the initial 220 IL apartments at The Gatesworth. From zero to 100 percent occupied in 23 months after opening. In hindsight, that was pretty darn good for a high-end, innovative living concept.

After getting to full occupancy at The Gatesworth, I turned my efforts toward third-party turnaround community consulting under the name One On One. I used these turnaround fill campaigns in part to see if what I learned about sales effectiveness while filling The Gatesworth would work for other sales teams in different settings. I also did it to pay off over $1.5 million of personal debt that I had run up to stay afloat while filling up The Gatesworth. With One On One, I also managed to create a viable consulting business.

In over a dozen of these turnaround campaigns, I committed myself to fill financially troubled communities within very short time frames of 90 to 120 days. I found that by fully immersing myself within the community and living on-site, I was able to better empathize with prospects. I got to quickly and authentically know the venues, programs, and services, as well as many of their residents and staff. This focused, hands-on experience was critical to my being able to deliver PCS with confidence. I aligned my objectives with the owners', and nearly all of my compensation was performance-based and tied to short-term occupancy gains. I never missed hitting one of my performance bonuses. I successfully repeated this process in communities across the US and Canada, with all kinds of financial models. They were also communities of various age, unit size, and pricing level, as well as various levels of hospitality, services, and care.

My current beliefs and PCS practices and the foundational workflows in Sherpa are deeply anchored in these One On One, hands-on selling successes. Together with my business partner, Alex Fisher, I built on the lessons described above to adapt and incorporate evidence-based techniques from the psychology of change models, identify key performance drivers, and establish time-oriented performance metrics. We have iteratively and continuously refined, field-tested, and enhanced the methodology over the past 30 years. Most recently, we have further tested and confirmed the efficacy of our PCS approach with extensive sales performance data from Sherpa.[19]

COUNTING WHAT COUNTS:
SHORTCOMINGS OF TRADITIONAL METRICS

Senior living industry conversion ratios have historically been defined as the number of prospects who move in versus the number of new prospects who inquire over a given period of time. In my experience, most senior living providers attempt to get more sales by generating more leads—sometimes hundreds more than they need.[20] The underlying limitation of speed-to-lead sellers is that they simply don't believe that by modifying your sales counselor behaviors, you can convert a lot more higher-functioning prospects like Mitch. A speed-to-lead approach

---

[19] For the most current edition of the Sherpa Sales Performance Data Report, visit https://sherpacrm.com/2020/08/06/from-the-data-team-covid-19-sales-performance-report-july update/?preview=true &_thumbnail_id=20876

[20] During the initial community data onboarding process, Sherpa guides a lead cleanup process. Using mutually agreeable filtering criteria, the community often substantially reduces the number of leads retained to far below industry averages. Nevertheless, a 2020 Sherpa data report showed that the average community using Sherpa had 14 active leads per vacant unit. A mere 7 percent conversion rate of these existing leads (with or without any new leads) would fill every vacant unit. *IBID note 24 above.*

doesn't identify leading performance indicators to account for the impact that you can get from an effective, proactive, evidence-based sales conversion process. A speed-to-lead approach assumes, instead, that key sales conversion ratios are fixed and inflexible; we just shouldn't expect to convert people like Mitch.

A speed-to-lead approach doesn't identify leading performance indicators to account for the impact that you can get from an effective, proactive, evidence-based sales conversion process.

From this perspective, the only way that transactional sellers can increase move-ins is by generating more initial tours with prospects who are forced to move somewhere. The working assumption is that more inquiries will generate more tours, which, in turn, is the only means to cultivate more move-ins. From this perspective, unfortunately, more vibrant prospects like Mitch who are not "urgent" are almost always quickly, easily, and unnecessarily ignored by a senior living sales team.

HOW TO MEASURE SUCCESS IN GETTING PROSPECTS "READY" TO BUY

Typical industry CRMs were designed to inform operators and investors about ongoing changes in occupancy based on the number of new leads/tours and an urgency-based pipeline of hot, warm, and cold leads. These performance metrics were clearly not designed by senior living sales professionals, nor were they intended to support and encourage more effective selling behaviors. As such, their data collection and reporting criteria are based on transactional, speed-to-lead metrics modeled after what works for skilled nursing homes, residential real estate, and multifamily sales scenarios.

The shortcomings of typical industry CRMs led Alex and me to reflect and ask ourselves, "What should we measure and manage to get higher visit-to-move-in ratios? Specifically, are there sales behaviors to be identified, tracked, and measured to assess progress toward a move-in decision?" We knew from personal, hands-on sales experience that building relationships with empathy greatly increases chances for a sale. However, we wanted to better understand how to measure the outcome and quality of prospect interactions. Those indicators would allow us to follow the prospect's decision-making journey and help us determine when a prospect was "ready" to explore a more solution-oriented selling process.

The result for us was Sherpa. Designed to guide and assist an emotional change process with state-of-the-art technology and data analytics, Sherpa is a comprehensive sales enablement platform that gives senior living professionals the tools and training needed to create an effective, dynamic, and sustainable sales culture. Developed and launched by Alex and me in June of 2014, Sherpa is a software as a service (SaaS) tool. It integrates PCS Stages of Change theory, results-oriented processes, and workflows into the core of a user-friendly, web-based solution.

Designed to guide and assist an emotional change process with state-of-the-art technology and data analytics, Sherpa is a comprehensive sales enablement platform that gives senior living professionals the tools and training needed to create an effective, dynamic, and sustainable sales culture.

Sherpa guides the user, usually a community-based sales counselor, through the sales process. Sherpa CRM brings the recording, aggregating, and reporting of user sales efforts together for better sales performance. Online and in-person courses on topics key to PCS success help the user build and sustain better conversions. Performance data from thousands of communities and millions of prospect interactions fuels business intelligence tools that make sales performance data accessible, meaningful, and actionable. Predictive artificial intelligence algorithms also allow us to continually enhance, update, and improve the PCS approach.

BEHAVIORS THAT DRIVE BETTER
VISIT-TO-MOVE-IN CONVERSIONS

W hat are the vital behaviors, activities, and outcomes that contribute to producing better visit-to-close ratios and incremental move-ins with higher-functioning prospects? Specifically, what drives higher visit-to-move-in conversion rates with otherwise qualified prospects that we typically set aside just because they aren't "ready"?

In *Moneyball*, author Michael Lewis illustrates how Oakland Athletics manager Billy Beane challenged the conventional model used by baseball insiders to evaluate success.[21] PCS could give senior living providers who rely solely on a transactional model a huge opportunity for increased sales. Once we began tracking and analyzing large pools of time- and outcome-oriented data with Sherpa, clear trends emerged. While senior living sales performance data has not yet reached the level of baseball statistical analytics, we do now have some innovative sales metrics that will forever change how we measure effectiveness. Not surprisingly, the answer, as considered more fully in the next chapters, involves consideration of selling time and how it is invested, along with positive outcomes (readiness advances) achieved.

1. Visit-to-Move-In Conversion Ratios

First, from a financial perspective, senior living sales success comes from:

---

[21] Billy Beane felt that statistics such as batting average and runs batted in (typically used to evaluate hitters) were misleading. Instead, statistical analysis demonstrated that on-base and slugging percentages were better indicators of offensive success because they correlated with total runs scored and games won. By analogy, this section considers indicators of sales success that include prospect advances that are not typically identified or valued by senior housing providers.

- Converting as many individual prospects to residents as possible.
- Minimizing discounts given.
- Maximizing anticipated length of stay.

Achieving incremental sales success turns on our ability to identify, track, and attain meaningful conversion-driving metrics. These are metrics that track the prospect's advances along a very personal readiness journey. Once a prospect is ready to make a logical buying decision, the probability of a sale and a move-in substantially increases.

There are two relevant conversion ratios used to gauge effectiveness in senior living sales. The first is the percentage of new inquiries with whom we are able to get initial face-to-face interactions, either at our community or in their homes. We call this the *inquiry-to-visit ratio.*[22] We believe that a more critical ratio, and one that is more difficult to achieve, is usually thought of as the percentage of move-ins from new prospects who have been face to face with us at least one time. We call this the *visit-to-move-in ratio.* Achieving a higher visit-to-move-in ratio is both more difficult and a lot more critical to increasing sales results, especially with higher-functioning prospects like Mitch.

Consider the impact of a prospect-centered approach on sales conversion rates by comparing sales conversion results.

---

[22] In calculating this ratio, "visits" include all initial face-to-face visits, whether by walk-in, tour, or home visit. We do not include repeat visits in the ratio. While repeat tours and home visits are an important part of the selling process, we do not view them as having any strategic or predictive value. Rather, they are viewed as only one of many tactics or sales behaviors that can be used to advance prospects toward a decision to move. Other commonly used tactics include participation at on-site educational or social events, attendance at scheduled resident events, trial stays, conversations and meetings with adult children and other decision influencers, and personalized CFU.

Sales Conversion Funnels: Industry, OOO Teams IL, and AL

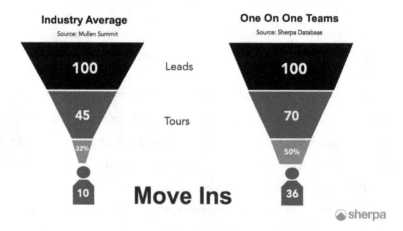

Here is the best information we have regarding the industry's average new-lead-to-move-in conversion ratio statistics.[23] For every 100 qualified leads that the typical community generates, 45 will agree to at least one tour or home visit ("visit"). Of those, only 10 will move in. That represents a 10 percent inquiry-to-move-in ratio and a 23 percent visit-or tour-to-move-in rate. I believe we can do better.

In terms of what's possible using PCS, the following is a summary of the conversion rates of the sales teams I led during eight One On One turnaround campaigns. We were able to achieve:

- 70 percent inquiry-to-visit ratio for IL and 75 percent for AL.
- 51 percent visit-to-move-in conversions for IL and 60 percent for AL communities.[24]

---

[23] Data compiled from more than 100 different IL and AL communities by NIC (NIC 2011 Regional Symposium; *Select Seniors* Housing Sales & Marketing Statistics) and presented by Tony Mullen at Annual Advanced Sales & Marketing Summit For Seniors Housing, December 2011. Margaret Wylde and ProMatura Group are conducting a new, more comprehensive industrywide study.

[24] Each of these eight turnaround campaigns represented three to four months of my personal hands-on PCS. The communities were located in the Midwest. Four of the campaigns were at IL communities, and four others were AL. During these eight campaigns, there were 808 IL units and 363 AL units leased. Two were initial fill campaigns from the time of opening, and two others were communities that were still in a fill mode two to three years after opening. Four other were at turnaround communities that had been opened more than 20 years earlier.

Thus, for every 100 leads, we converted 35.7 IL and 45 AL prospects, many times more than the 10 converted by typical IL/AL communities. Coming from a vision of changing the way that senior living sells, our challenge was that while we could fill our own communities and turnaround sites where we could oversee, participate in, and direct the selling process, we did not have the tools to scale PCS. Beginning in mid-2014, that changed with the launch of the Sherpa sales enablement platform. Even average performers in the Sherpa database today see much better visit-to-move-in results than a typical speed-to-lead community. For every 100 leads, 55 will visit[25] and 20 will move in, which is a 20 percent inquiry-to-move-in ratio and a 36 percent visit-to-move-in ratio. Again, that's double the number of move-ins achieved by typical industry speed-to-lead sellers.

Sales Funnel Analysis comparing Industry Average to Average Sherpa Performers

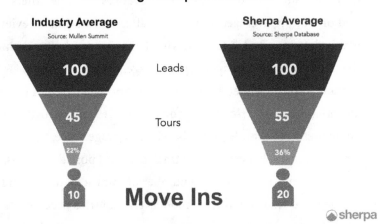

Industry Average
Source: Mullen Summit

Sherpa Average
Source: Sherpa Database

100 — Leads — 100

45 — Tours — 55

22% — 36%

10 — **Move Ins** — 20

sherpa

---

[25] Note: these top Sherpa performers achieve a 10 percent greater than average effectiveness in getting new prospects to visit. That is in part because of formulation. In Sherpa, we only count sales-qualified leads, a new inquiry who has connected first with a sales counselor. That means we generally have a smaller lead pool for an equal number of visits. Also, our numbers are typically higher since within "visits" we include both initial tours as well as initial home visits, not just tours. Again, we don't count clearly unqualified leads and increase the number of face-to-face interactions by adding both tours and home visits.

PCS helps sales professionals broaden the sales funnel at the lower end, often by more effective strategies to help more of the existing "cold" prospects get ready.

2. Vital Behaviors that Drive Higher Visit-to-Move-In Conversions

In terms of really scaling PCS to larger-portfolio companies and beyond the US, we concluded that an important question remained: could we identify the vital behaviors and outcomes that predict better visit-to-close ratios with higher-functioning prospects? If so, instead of just counting and tracking the number of inquiries or number of sales interactions, we could focus on measuring and promoting *more effective* interactions.

For us, a vital behavior is a high-leverage action that will directly lead to the results that drive readiness advances.[26] While others were fixated on batting average, Billy Beane, after an exhaustive review of available data, concluded that the vital behavior of a batter is simply, "on-base percentage and slugging percentage. Everything else is far less important."[27] Beane risked his career on adopting a new and different set of performance metrics. He was determined to create a better, more accurate method for professional baseball to gauge success.

Transactional sellers count and track pre- and post-tour status, perceived prospect urgency, and the number of sales activities. With PCS, we reimagined traditional sales models and metrics used across the country for predicting, monitoring, and measuring effective performance Prior to the launch of Sherpa, we had data, but only in the form of handwritten records of what it took to generate our own incredible

---

[26] Patterson, K, et al. *Influencer: The Power to Change Anything.* McGraw-Hill, 2008.

[27] Lewis, Michael. *Moneyball: the Art of Winning an Unfair Game.* W.W. Norton, 2013.

conversion rates. From these records, it became clear to us that the amount and allocation of time invested in connecting, engaging, planning, and following up is a reliable proxy to gauge the level of prospect connection and engagement and the probability of advancement.

With PCS, we reimagined traditional sales models and metrics used across the country for predicting, monitoring, and measuring effective performance.

Here, then, are the key measurable and experience-tested factors critical to driving higher visit-to-move-in conversions:

- *Amount of direct sales engagement, or TSZ.*
- *Time per lead worked: the average time invested in each lead worked (total TSZ divided by total leads worked during time frame) is perhaps the most reliable indicator of sales success.*
- *Allocation of TSZ in planning strategic and tactical next steps to advance the readiness of individual prospects.*
- *Use of high-impact tactics.*
  - *Home visits.*
  - *Purposeful, personalized CFU.*
  - *Organizational tactic: make the ED the sales leader.*

PCS Leading Performance Drivers

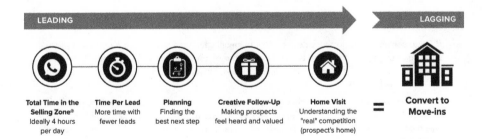

| Total Time in the Selling Zone® Ideally 4 hours per day | Time Per Lead More time with fewer leads | Planning Finding the best next step | Creative Follow-Up Making prospects feel heard and valued | Home Visit Understanding the "real" competition (prospect's home) | Convert to Move-ins |

Collectively, these are the key factors that account for converting double the number of people that visit.[28] Each of these factors is focused on the customer's journey toward a willingness to buy or readiness.[29] Each provides a strong predictor of sales success. The following chapters will examine each of these key factors in more detail. But first and foremost, let's explore the amount and nature of the selling time needed to help individual prospects get ready to move.

---

[28] Other contributing factors include the extent of meaningful discovery, getting a prospect's photo, direct sales engagement from the ED, and the number of advances along the readiness continuum. Ongoing examination of Sherpa data will make it possible for us to continue to refine, clarify, and fine-tune these factors.

[29] "Too often, sellers think activities such as giving presentations, making sales calls, or submitting proposals constitute the major milestones of a sales strategy. While these activities are important to making a sale, they are inadequate if they are not balanced with some measure of milestone which memorializes the customers' perspectives." (Huthwaite Asia Pacific, founded by Neil Rackham, *Pipeline Management*, http://www.huthwaite.com.au/pipeline-management.html)

CHAPTER 4

It's About Time in the
Selling Zone

It's really clear that the most precious resource we all have is time.

—Steve Jobs

What I found in the sales trenches is that to enhance performance, you need to purposefully invest time to build relationships and uncover emotional blocks. In other words, invest time to facilitate buying before even thinking about selling, offering solutions, or closing. It takes a lot of time—you need to laser focus what precious little you have on one prospect at a time!

> Invest time to facilitate buying before even thinking about selling, offering solutions, or closing.

TIME IN THE SELLING ZONE

When I was first practicing law, the most valuable thing I learned was that as a professional advocate, the client's interests come first. When I left the practice of law and transitioned to senior living, that fundamental truth stayed the same. I've always wanted to help people, to be their advocate, and I'm grateful that some of the same characteristics that made me successful as a lawyer became the foundation for what we call PCS.

Take, for instance, the idea of tracking time. Yes, there's a common joke that attorneys are always "on the clock." But when I became a senior housing sales professional, I understood early on that my time was my most valuable and limited resource. Once I began leading sales teams, I started tracking their focused sales time against their results. That simple relationship became a key to our success: the more time we invested in focused sales efforts, the more successful we became.[30] That truth became the foundation of investing TSZ.

That simple relationship became a key to our success: the more time we invested on focused sales efforts, the more successful we became. That truth became the foundation of investing TSZ.

The emptiness of a typical "the more leads, tours, and call-outs, the better" approach in senior living sales is illustrated by an extensive study of time-oriented performance metrics taken from Sherpa user data. The initial study was conducted in 2016 by ProMatura Group[31] and has been supplemented with subsequent Sherpa internal studies. Taken together, these studies identified distinct sales behaviors that are proven to drive and help predict higher conversions. Stated simply, it's about investing more TSZ with fewer prospects.

A commonsense conclusion validated in the ProMatura study data is that sales teams do increase sales conversion rates by investing more time in direct selling. Not surprising. Spending more TSZ with prospects and

---

[30] It assumes that the relevant factor to measure is time invested, not activities. Per Rackham, "In small sales it is generally desirable to keep the transaction time short; in larger sales—for a whole variety of reasons—a shorter transaction time has few advantages and many penalties." (1998, p. 33).

[31] The study's initial phase, conducted by the ProMatura Group, examined 302,159 interactions of 502 senior living salespeople nationwide with 23,480 leads at 41 communities offering IL, 71 communities offering AL services, and 75 communities providing MC, between January 1 and December 31, 2015. The results of this study were published in a Sherpa Senior Housing News white paper, *Sales Enablement in Senior Living: A Roadmap to an Effective and Sustainable Sales Culture*, a copy of which can be obtained at https://resources.seniorhousingnews.com/a-roadmap-to-an-effective-and-sustainable-sales-culture Sponsored by ASHA. ProMatura is near completion of a second and more extensive study of Sherpa data, titled *The Art and Science of Sales in Age-Qualified Housing*, which will be published by ASHA in 2020. The second phase will look at further segmenting the initial gross data into multiple categories such as community size, age, levels of care, geography, and so on.

their families allows for more meaningful interactions. The prospect may eventually be open to hearing our solutions, but only after trust is gained. The approach itself differentiates our community from the competition and creates a compelling reason for the prospect to choose our community.

How many selling hours did it take to convert prospects who did move in? Our initial study shows it took about 10 hours in TSZ for AL prospects and about 20 hours for IL rental prospects. Note that the time available to invest in TSZ for any particular community is a limited resource. We have found that only about half the time spent at work can actually be spent in the Selling Zone. That is because, when done well, connecting and untangling prospect fears is emotionally exhausting work for the counselors. Moreover, even in the most productive sales offices, there are still various tasks, meetings, and non-sales activities that need tending to.[32] Therefore, the amount of total selling time available is a critical factor driving sales success. Assuming that the typical sales counselor generates 50 percent of their working hours in the Selling Zone for 22 eight-hour days, each counselor has only about 88 hours in the Selling Zone available each month. That's it. So it is essential that we use those precious hours to our greatest benefit.

Activities Included in the Time in the Selling Zone Calculation

But it wasn't just the *amount* of time that mattered. We also found that *how* we spent that time was equally as important. In law, I spent a great deal of time building case studies for my clients and any relevant subject

---

[32] Time spent in the Selling Zone for the first half of 2020 was, due to COVID-19, down 21 percent from the 2019 average. Sales teams worked 10 percent fewer leads than the 2019 average and spent 20 percent fewer hours in the Selling Zone. One explanation for the reduction in selling hours might be that COVID-19 brought all hands on deck to monitor for infections; source, purchase, and distribute personal protective equipment; continuously clean and disinfect; and be a source of understanding and support for our residents and their families.

matter. Time was dedicated to research. My approach was planned carefully after weighing multiple options. I was overprepared in every instance. In sales, I realized that time invested in *planning* a conversation or interaction and following up after was not considered to be "selling." Yet from experience, I found that individualized planning to establish a strategy to advance a specific prospect was just as valuable in terms of closing as time spent in a conversation or interaction. The more well-informed my teams and I were, the more prepared we were to be present in our interactions with prospects, and the better we performed.

> The more well-informed my teams and I were, the more prepared we were to be present in our interactions with prospects, and the better we performed.

In law, once you spend the time on research and planning, you craft a strategy for your approach. Then you identify tactics that execute vital elements of that strategy. How does that apply to sales? We invest time in our prospects. We remain curious, challenging assumptions and exploring motivators and fears to find out all that we can about who this person is and where they are on an individual readiness journey. As their guides through a major life transition, we craft a strategy to help them untangle the unresolved emotional obstacles on their path. Our strategy may be something like, "Build trust by evoking stories that reveal their life story." Our tactic may be, "Visit their home to explore a family photo album."

From this perspective, we realized we needed to redefine what key activities constituted direct selling time. Senior living operators consider time invested in every area of their business other than sales: housekeeping, nursing, personal care, food services, transportation, etc. They also generally track the calendar days that it takes from inquiry to move-in but, surprisingly, not the factors that might accelerate that time frame.

Most operators think of a sales counselor's time spent on marketing, advertising, or events as selling time. In addition, they include time spent on activities or tasks that are operational in nature. These are tasks like move-in coordination, new resident orientation, and helping with resident or prospect gathering. While assisting in marketing or operations is necessary sometimes, those activities do not drive higher sales conversions. It was obvious that we needed a new definition of direct selling time.

We coined "Time in the Selling Zone" to include the time invested in individual prospects for engagements that are:

- Face to face directly with the prospect or their family members
- Voice to voice (plus all non-face-to-face prospect engagements such as email, text messaging, or mail)
- Time spent planning before or after prospect engagements, including exploring life stories through conversations and internet research, assessing readiness, and thinking about best next steps
- Time invested in creating personalized, creative prospect follow-up

More Time Per Lead Worked

The ProMatura study also concluded that *spending more time with fewer prospects* is what most drives higher sales conversions. This finding, while new to the senior living industry, is consistent with what leading sales research is finding outside of our industry. For example, Ryan Fuller, CEO and co-founder of VoloMetrix, a leading people analytics company acquired by Microsoft in 2015, studied the sales force of a large B2B software company using six quarters of quota attainment data for several thousand employees. In part, he concluded, "Death trumps breadth—top sellers focus on building deeper relationships with fewer customers rather than casting a wider net

> *"Death trumps breadth—top sellers focus on building deeper relationships with fewer customers rather than casting a wider net of shallow engagements."*

Time in the Selling Zone

MARKETING

- ✓ Events
- ✓ Ad Placement
- ✓ Bulk Mailings
- ✓ E-mail Campaigns
- ✓ PR
- ✓ Outreach
- ✓ Social Media
- ✓ Etc.

SALES

VOICE TO VOICE

FACE TO FACE

PLANNING

CREATIVE FOLLOW-UP

OPERATIONS

- ✓ Move-in/Move-out
- ✓ Unit Readiness
- ✓ Ops Meetings
- ✓ Resident Satisfaction
- ✓ Paperwork
- ✓ Etc.

of shallow engagements. They spend 18% more time with customers... yet interact with 40% fewer accounts allowing them more time with each one."[33]

We knew that this was true for senior living sales from years of hands-on selling and from our theoretical Stages of Change model. We were curious. Does data prove that increasing the average time spent with each prospect has a direct, quantifiable, and observable impact on visit- (tour) or move-in conversions? An internal Sherpa study looked at results across a broad section of the Sherpa customer base for a total of 512 communities. Each of these customers had been using Sherpa for over 12 months. Here's what we found: those communities that spent one hour or less per prospect averaged a 21 percent visit-to-move-in ratio. In contrast, the communities that spent an average of two and a half hours or more with each prospect improved sales results by an astounding 90–100 percent.

Those communities that spent one hour or less per prospect worked averaged a 21 percent visit-to-move-in ratio. In contrast, the communities that spent an average of two and a half hours or more with each prospect improved sales results by an astounding 90–100 percent.

Impact of Time Spent on Conversion Rates

It takes time to make emotional connections, build trust, and help prospects get ready. Since time is a limiting factor, how can you increase

---

[33] "What Makes Great Salespeople." *Harvard Business Review*, 2015.

the time invested per prospect? First, you can delegate non-sales activities. Anything that's not directly related to selling and getting the prospect across the readiness gap, like move-in coordination or event planning, can easily be done by somebody else at a much lower expense.

While counterintuitive, reducing the number of leads is a second way to get more TSZ.

While counterintuitive, reducing the number of leads is a second way to get more TSZ. How many leads are enough? In a stabilized community, you don't need more than 10 to 15 leads for every vacant unit—even with average industry visit-to-move-in conversion rates. If you have more leads than that, and most providers do, processing, qualifying, and working on that many leads reduces the time you have left to spend in the Selling Zone. Don't bulk up on leads. It doesn't help you or your prospects. Regardless of how many active leads you have, top performers can really only focus intensely on about 10 prospects at a time. They try to generate lots of small steps or advances with each, one small step after another. They do this over and over again. The key to a successful sales marathon approach is to "close" on the smallest possible advance in the sale as soon as it becomes possible.

Adding more sales counselors or administrative support staff is a third way to invest more TSZ I can remember the days when there were no counselors and it was all on the ED to both sell and operate the building. Now, most communities have dedicated salespeople and some notion of a team. Within the sales team and between sales and operational teams, establish a supportive, cooperative sales culture. Team selling is a tremendous advantage for discovery, tour logistics, journaling, and planning personalized follow up and next steps. In the senior living sales environment, where overall market penetration is only 10 percent, there is simply no advantage to forcing selling counselors to compete with each other. Set up common sales performance milestones for the community (versus for individual sales team members), and incentivize the team when they reach those milestones. In other words, pay incentives (albeit in differing amounts) to everyone when anyone on the selling team gets a lease. Team-based incentives are the first step to ensure that everyone feels free to share leads, ideas, honest feedback, and information. Use a team approach to review the background, key motivators, and sales history and to develop personalized action plans for the team's top prospects.

During face-to-face presentations to seniors (tours, home visits, and even voice-to-voice conversations), two sales professionals are often more effective than one. Prospects seldom explore senior living without spouses, adult children, or other key decision influencers. While filling a community in Provo, Utah, we had a prospect come with their entire extended family, 47 people in all. Imagine trying to get discovery or take them on a tour with only one sales counselor. And to improve results, it doesn't just have to be two leasing counselors. It could be a leasing counselor joined by an ED, regional manager, chef, receptionist, resident, or any department head.

Here are a few reasons two counselors are more effective than one:

- Dedicating two sales counselors makes a strong statement about how important each prospect is to your community.
- Two heads are better than one. There is an enhanced ability to listen, observe, and respond to prospect concerns both during and after the presentation.
- There is more opportunity to create a more meaningful tour experience. One counselor can stick with the prospect while the other checks on available apartments, reserves a lunch table, enlists assistance from key staff members, or works with accompanying children or other decision influencers.

How the Best Performers Allocate TSZ

For the most part, senior living sales leaders have the ability to prioritize and focus the selling time available. That time prioritization can be guided by the ProMatura study of Sherpa sales metrics. We looked at the relative impact of certain activities, behaviors, and practices on increasing conversion rates. The ProMatura data proves that increasing the number of sales conversions of higher-functioning senior living prospects is all about investing more time. The ProMatura study shows that it takes an average of 10 hours of TSZ to help an assisted living (AL) prospect get ready to buy. For IL prospects, it takes 20 hours to get to the same result. The time spent is even longer for the typical CCRC.

Whatever amount of TSZ you have available, using it to hunt for urgency can be counterproductive. The most urgent prospects usually have the shortest length of stay, and they typically require more time and attention from our administrative and care staff. When higher-functioning prospects see high-acuity residents sitting in the lobby, it often reinforces preconceived negative feelings toward senior housing. Our study shows that instead, it's more effective to invest as much time as possible cultivating prospect readiness. Not surprisingly, our study showed that the longer each prospect engagement is, whether it's on the phone or in person, the more likely it is that the person will convert and move in.

In terms of the relative impact that various sales activity drivers have on performance, top performers from the Sherpa database invest 35 percent of their time in face-to-face interactions, 30 percent in planning, 20 percent in phone or email conversations, and 15 percent in CFU.

In terms of the relative impact that various sales activity drivers have on performance, top performers from the Sherpa database invest 35 percent of their time in face-to-face interactions, 30 percent in planning, 20 percent in phone or email conversations, and 15 percent in CFU.

Best Sherpa Performers

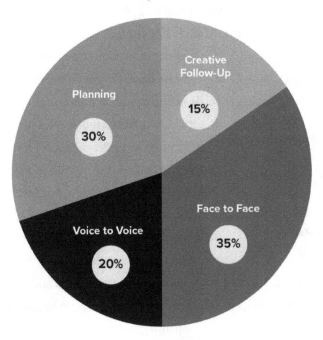

Note that about 45 percent of the best sales performers' time is spent just on planning next steps and personalized CFU. Many salespeople, however, have been trained to offer product-centered solutions and to try to "close" as often and as soon as possible. Unfortunately, this type of surface fishing doesn't involve much time planning or CFU. Top Sherpa performers average 120 minutes on CFU for each IL prospect who moves in.

Top Sherpa performers average 120 minutes on CFU for each IL prospect who moves in.

An interesting thing we learned from the study is that the number of call-ins to top performers was a whopping seven and a half times greater than call-outs. A good rule of thumb is to think about what is required to generate a call-in from an existing prospect and always try to do more of that.

In every respect, the approach should be thoughtful, purposeful, and *actionable*. If the strategy isn't working, by all means, we pivot. If the tactic backfires, we immediately try another one. But we never stop progressing in our knowledge of the prospect and in our desire to participate in a genuine relationship with them. From my journey as an attorney to becoming a sales professional, my core purpose hasn't changed: I want to help people and become their guide, whether or not they ever decide to move, and even if they decide to move somewhere else.

From my journey as an attorney to becoming a sales professional, my core purpose hasn't changed: I want to help people and become their guide, whether or not they ever decide to move, and even if they decide to move somewhere else.

Regardless, sales counselors must understand that prospects are looking for guidance, trust, and a safe place to voice their motivation, fears, and aspirations for the future. Understand that prospects don't want to be sold to; rather, they need help and guidance to buy. Believe that you can help prospects get ready when you are able to inspire, facilitate, and assist them in the work of addressing their emotional barriers to change. Your chances of succeeding increase with the investment of quality TSZ.

Your chances of succeeding increase with the investment of quality TSZ.

CONCLUSION

I n our industry, top sellers spend more time working with each lead. They invest nearly 50 percent of that time in planning before each prospect interaction and in doing personalized CFU afterward. They shift the target from a focus on velocity to one of planning and purposeful deliberation.[34] They also create intermediate prospect outcome targets along the way, from inquiry to close.

It's about time. If you invest TSZ, your senior living sales results will improve. You can identify, track, set goals, and focus on improving the key sales behaviors that have been proven to increase sales results. In the end, you win. Your community and company win. But perhaps even more important, a prospect-centered perspective will help enhance the lives of many of the 90 percent of senior adults who fearfully cling to their houses and to lifestyles that no longer fit their needs. That's heroic selling.

It's about time. If you invest TSZ, your senior living sales results will improve. You can identify, track, set goals, and focus on improving the key sales behaviors that have been proven to increase sales results. In the end, you win. Your community and company win. But perhaps even more important, a prospect-centered perspective will help enhance the lives of many of the 90 percent of senior adults who fearfully cling to their houses and to lifestyles that no longer fit their needs. That's heroic selling.

In search of a model for how sales counselors can engage the TSZ they have available, PCS led to the identification of three distinct selling processes that leasing counselors use to advance readiness. Simply, they are connect, untangle, and then advance. The following chapters will explore this three-phase process.

---

[34] Homburg et al. (2011) point out that implementing a customer orientation and adapting each sales presentation to the needs of the customer instead of using a one-size-fits-all style presentation requires a lot of time. Salespeople who spend more time per customer reduce the total number of customers they can serve. Nevertheless, Homburg et al. conclude that investing more time per customer is justified for businesses like seniors housing, "which offer highly individualized products, products which are of greater importance to their customers, and that are positioned at a higher price point."

CHAPTER 5

Connect and Build Trust with Empathy

Empathy is simply listening, holding space, withholding judgment, emotionally connecting, and communicating that incredibly healing message of you're not alone.

—Brené Brown

CONNECTING WITH CURIOSITY AND CARING

Have you ever gotten stuck with prospects who aren't ready? Consider the higher-functioning, financially qualified prospects you've gotten to know personally. They are people like Mitch who you are confident would lead better lives in a community like yours. But they're also the ones who, after an initial round of activity fails to produce a sale, are typically classified as cold leads. Higher-functioning prospects say no or "I'm not ready yet" nearly all of the time, regardless of how much they would benefit from a move.

Ask 1,000 qualified senior adults about moving into an age-segregated senior living community. Over 900 will tell you that they intend to remain in their own houses, condos, or apartments until they die or until failing health forces them to move. For today's seniors, moving into congregate housing is a "postponable" decision. In most cases, they won't even discuss underlying resistance until you have developed a strong personal, non-business relationship. Your challenge is to gain enough credibility, intimacy, connection, and trust so that the prospect will share the real issues they confront.

Successful senior living sales counselors convert more prospects by motivating the prospect to confront their own emotional resistance than by trying to change the prospect's perception of the facts.[35] According to Solie's *How to Say it to Seniors*,[36] "The elderly feel a need to say NO! that comes from deep within, because when everything around them seems to be giving way, sometimes the only control they can exercise is to say NO! Anything we say that erodes what little they still control can be met with almost irrational resistance." Prospect rejection is the norm. Our hands-on experience and Sherpa data confirm that trying to convince or persuade a senior prospect, at least those who still have a choice about whether to move, will only get you to no faster.

The highest-performing counselors, the heroic ones, know how to invest the time needed to empathically connect and confront emotional resistance before trying to offer solutions or otherwise sell features and benefits. Senior living sales teams become more effective when they are taught and trained in the art and science of connection.

CASE STUDY: MARY

Mary was an IL prospect who toured our community. We also visited her at her home, a fairly large two-story house with an English Tudor façade, four bedrooms, and a large, beautifully landscaped yard. Although she and her recently deceased

---

[35] Wylde, M. A., and D. A. Smith. " Factors Associated with Successful Sales Presentations of Independent Living, Assisted Living, and Continuing Care Retirement Communities." *Seniors Housing & Care Journal*, 2004, pp. 12–25.

[36] Solie, David. *How to Say It to Seniors Closing the Communication Gap with Our Elders*. Prentice Hall Press, 2004.

husband had raised her daughter Susan there, Mary now lived alone. She was 86 and still driving, but Susan was not so sure she should be.

Susan really wanted her mom to move to a retirement community. Nearly all of Mary's friends had died or fallen out of touch over the years. Her social network was shrinking. She was forgetting to take her meds. She had a laundry room in the basement, and Mary was afraid of falls. Once a great cook, Mary was now eating TV dinners at home alone. Mary said her life had turned into a cocoon.

A transactional seller would begin by examining Mary's problems, vulnerabilities, and maladies. That way they could be matched to a community's features and amenities. The intention of the transactional seller is to convince or persuade Mary that she would be better off moving to their community than she would be if she were to stay home. Clearly, Mary would be better off by moving. Senior living offers tremendous benefits such as socialization and nutritious food with no grocery shopping, cooking, or cleaning. It offers convenient chauffeured transportation, minimizes the risk of falls, and can help with medication management.

All of these benefits would have enhanced Mary's quality of life. But she was not emotionally ready to buy. She said that even thinking about a move made her come to terms with the fact of her age and dying. "Moving out of my home felt like a 'final' move," she said. "And after giving up my family home, who would I become?" There was simply no way to overcome or argue Mary into being ready. The kind of persuasion that worked when I was selling houses did not help me here.

Assuming that the typical industry sales counselor can collect as much relevant discovery about Mary as we do, the challenge with a speed-to-lead approach is that there is simply not enough available time to engage in trust-building. Yet without sufficient time, how will you be able to connect and help Mary and many other cold prospects confront their fears and untangle their emotional resistance?

Facilitate Readiness through Conversation and Connection

Resistance for Mary and other higher-functioning prospects is organically linked to their core values and their internal decision-making process. Taking on Mary's perspective with empathy rather than sympathy helps us build connections based on trust. Establishing Mary's trust gives us confidence that will help Mary unravel the origins of her underlying resistance. From a prospect-centered perspective, it's discouraging to everyone involved if we focus our attention on offering solutions for a disability, chronic illness, or vulnerability. We are a lot more effective at "selling" when we set aside our own egos as sales counselors and give up the quest to close the deal. In short, until someone is ready to even consider moving, *stop selling.* Connect. The most effective way to do our jobs in this industry is to empathically and compassionately inspire connection and conversation.

As sales counselors, when we "stop selling," we set aside our role as a "salesperson." We suspend our drive to meet quotas, close deals, increase occupancy, and earn incentives. We are left to give up typical sales results and adapt to a new role that is more like a counselor, advocate, or life coach—these are attributes of heroic selling. PCS is driven by an energetic and well-trained helping instinct. All of the pressure is on the sales counselor, not the prospect.

It's not easy to give up the sales result. It requires us to be present, authentic, and vulnerable. For a senior living sales counselor, that provokes our own internal resistance, especially when culturally in the US, vulnerability is most often associated with weakness. But as the best sales counselors come to learn, "vulnerability is not winning or losing: it's having the courage to show up and be seen when we have no control over the outcome. Vulnerability is not weakness; it's our greatest measure of courage."[37] Vulnerability reduces tension and promotes connection and trust.

Meaningful connections begin with what Brian Grazer calls a "curiosity conversation."[38] While it is important to plan and be prepared for each prospect conversation, Grazer says "it is even more important to show up with the capacity for wonderment and openness, a beginner's mind, really... with no [sales] endpoint in mind. That's what makes them conversations rather than rigid, agenda-driven interviews."

As the best sales counselors come to learn, "vulnerability is not winning or losing: it's having the courage to show up and be seen when we have no control over the outcome. Vulnerability is not weakness; it's our greatest measure of courage."

Like most people, Mary has stories to tell. She has an ideal concept of who she always thought she was or aspired to be: a therapist, author, and career woman. Encouraging Mary to tell us her life story and listening, being curious, validating, and aligning what we hear builds trust that paves the way for her to envision a new identity untangled from the past.

Each relationship develops in its own special way. When you begin to interact with a new prospect, chances are that your personalities and styles will be very different. To convert effectively, you first need to identify how your prospect wants to be approached and communicated with. Then you can adjust your body language, tone, and content to put them at ease.

Emotional resistance to moving creates tension and inhibits decision-making and action. Whether you are communicating face to face, voice to voice, or with a personalized CFU, adopt a style and format

---

[37] Brown Brené. *Rising Strong*. Vermilion, 2015, p. 4.

[38] Grazer, Brian. *Face to Face: the Art of Human Connection*. Simon Shuster, 2019, p. 22.

that reduces tension and motivates your prospect to act. For serious prospects, be serious. If your relationship or the prospect's personality invites humor, try to make the prospect laugh.

Try to match your style to your prospect's personality. Jim Cathcart,[39] author of *Relationship Selling*, illustrates how each of us thinks and makes decisions differently. Concentrate on how they make decisions— spontaneously or slowly and deliberately? Based on what they think or what others may think? Based more on feelings or facts? Then, adjust your style to communicate and sell *at the pace* and in the *style* that best suit them. Cathcart breaks typical personalities and decision-making styles into four types:

- **Interactive Socializer:** More playful, creative, and spontaneous. Loves variety; hates routine or ordinary. Responds to stimulation and the big picture. Throw in some quotes or stories about well-known or notable people associated with your community.
- **Cautious Thinker:** Tends to be in detail-oriented professions. Respects formality and detail. Be methodical. Construct logical reasoning. Support your arguments with facts and figures. Send an agenda with a visit or meeting invite. After a conversation or engagement, send a summary, statistics, or a worksheet.
- **Confident Director:** Likes to be in charge. Wants clear options with supporting information. Prefers to dictate the process. Follow their lead as to the nature, timing, and relevance of issues. Be direct and to the point.
- **Steady Relator:** Goes slow. Values stability and the status quo. Needs ongoing reassurance and nurturing. Tell stories, and use poems, personalized newsletters, and analogies. Talk about how others decided whether to move or stay.

---

[39] Cathcart, Jim. *Relationship Selling: Eight Competencies of Top Sales Producers.* Advantage Quest Publications, 2005.

The common thread is to personalize both the style as well as the content of engagements for maximum impact. More than anything else, attempting to mirror the prospect's communication approach (in conversations, during a visit, or when returning letters or responding to a video message with one of your own) fosters connection and trust.

The common thread is to personalize both the style as well as the content of engagements for maximum impact. More than anything else, attempting to mirror the prospect's communication approach (in conversations, during a visit, or when returning letters or responding to a video message with one of your own) fosters connection and trust.

Despite struggling with her health, Mary is by nature a Confident Director. Aging has challenged her self-confidence. With just a few purposeful, open-ended questions, we can begin to help her explore stories associated with her confidence in the past. For example, we learned that Mary was the first in her family to graduate college with a degree in clinical social work. That took confidence. She counseled hundreds of people as a clinical social worker, and for most of them, this included helping them regain confidence. Mary retired early from her clinical practice to help her husband run his residential real estate office. That took a leap of faith and, again, a sense of confident expectations.

Now, as she considers entering another new chapter, she is a mother, grandmother, and aspiring photographer. None of those roles was working very well, but still, Mary was torn. Ambivalent. If she stayed in her house, what would become of her? If she moved, who would she become? She was afraid to leave her home and did not easily accept encouragement to navigate this emotionally difficult transition. Her declining circumstances made her resist her otherwise confident approach to life.

With an empathic connection, we can help prospects like Mary recontextualize their life story around their ideal self and the person they would like to become during their next chapter. Connection to key life stories gave Mary an awareness of her authentic nature as master of her own fate. We helped Mary retell and reflect on stories of how she confronted barriers in the past, how she used her social work skills to help others, and how she might be able to confront new barriers now. Her logical alternatives remained the same as they were before we connected, but with her trust, we helped her reassess her own resistance. In the end, with some encouragement from us, Mary did take control of her own decision and chose to move in spite of her fear and resistance to change.

Build Trust

We invested quite a bit of time to build up Mary's trust in us. It was well worth the effort. Most sales counselors, however, tend to avoid personal trust-building and start instead with the benefits of what they're selling: the community and its venues, programs, and services. Most list features, floor plans, and monthly prices before they ever attempt to connect or build trust with the prospect. Does the following exchange sound familiar?

Prospect: Hello. I'm calling about my mom. We're getting worried because she's been falling and having trouble taking meds. I'm looking for more information.

Sales Counselor: Great! How old is she? What's wrong with her that prompted you to call? Now, let me tell you what we have.

Without any emotional connection, this response can come across as scheming, arrogant, or, worst of all, "feature dumping." This is what happens when we just start listing our services and amenities. As we're boasting our community's credentials, the prospect or her adult child is thinking, "This person cares more about themselves than they do about me. Why would I ever buy from them?"

Let's return to Mary. Later on, after she had moved into one of our communities, we asked, "What was the decision-making process like for you?"

"It was very scary," she said. "This kind of change is like climbing a mountain. I didn't know how or even if I could do it. Transition is not about moving from one place to another. It's about learning to let go. To accept that things are never going to be the way they were before."

We can provide guidance and counsel prospects like Mary if—and only if—they trust us to guide them. Studies show that people decide within seconds of meeting someone whether they're trustworthy or not. We answer by sensing a person's warmth, intentions, and empathic concern. This is an assessment based on an emotional connection rather than an assessment of professional skills or smarts.

> *Studies show that people decide within seconds of meeting someone whether they're trustworthy or not. We answer by sensing a person's warmth, intentions, and empathic concern.*

"If someone you're trying to influence doesn't trust you, you're not going to get very far," Amy Cuddy writes.[40] "In fact, you might even elicit suspicion because you come across as manipulative. You might have great ideas, but without trust, those ideas are impotent."

We believe that trust is the most important factor in the buying decision. Trust means that the other person believes you care about them, that you'll act with integrity, and that you have their best interests at heart. As Stephen Covey writes, "Trust is the glue of life. It's the most essential ingredient in effective communication. It's the foundational principle that holds all relationships."[41]

---

[40] Casselberry, Cuddy Amy Joy. *Presence: Bringing Your Boldest Self to Your Biggest Challenges.* Back Bay Books, 2018.

[41] Covey, Steven, et al.. *First Things First.* Franklin Covey, 1995 p.203

Trust is the glue of life. It's the most essential ingredient in effective communication. It's the foundational principle that holds all relationships.

Trust is the intimate space we create with—and for—another person so we can both experience a sense of belonging. It is built through meaningful, real conversations that form an authentic connection. Prospects need a safe space where they can express honest feelings and concerns without the fear of being "sold to." They won't care about your community and its benefits until they feel safe and trust you as a person. If you open your heart and focus on connecting with the prospect, you can help them feel seen and valued and nurture a sense of belonging.

Trust isn't just nice to have—it's essential to a successful sales effort.

Trust isn't just nice to have—it's essential to a successful sales effort. Trust, however, does not guarantee an outcome. We all know that in senior living sales, there are no guaranteed outcomes and plenty of uncertainty. Without trust, however, a prospect will put up emotional walls. They will make objections that, when taken literally, make no sense. Lacking trust, the next steps remain hidden and obscure.

STRATEGIES FOR BUILDING TRUST

Trust develops over time, and it won't happen on its own. You'll need to take the initiative. For trust to develop, you must proactively work at building it. Here are some strategies for doing so.

1. Start with you.

Why should your prospects trust you if you don't have trust in yourself? Have confidence in your skills and abilities to assess readiness, and then guide prospects in making their own decisions. Whether they buy from you or not, trusting in yourself helps you maintain confidence through the tumultuous sales process.

To be effective in guiding prospects, sales counselors must have the emotional intelligence to regulate their own ego and emotions. Even if it doesn't come naturally, senior living sales counselors can learn to actively listen. They can attempt to truly understand emotional resistance. Like true heroes, the best senior living counselors are nonjudgmental and sincerely curious, and they put their whole self into the effort of helping prospects overcome emotional resistance. *"And because each relationship builds and develops in its own unique and special way, there just aren't a lot of rules to follow. How do you let each and every prospect know how much you care? Well, you have to be amazing and outrageous. You have to be surprising and unpredictable and most of all you have to be there over and over again for that particular prospect."*[42] This takes patience, planning, and determination on the part of the sales counselor as well as those who manage them.

Be aware of your level of emotional quotient (EQ).[43] This includes the ability to identify and self-regulate your own fears and anxieties, such as:

- Fear of rejection or failure to meet goals or quotas.
- Fear of getting too close or even intimate with prospects who, 90 percent of the time, will reject you and just stay home.

---

[42] In reaction to the passive, order-taking sales process that characterized our industry at the time, in 1995, I authored and published *Guerilla Sales Tool Kit—Senior Housing Edition*. It drew from the work of J. Conrad Levinson and included a series of booklets, audio tapes, and templates. It also included the following observation: "When I say guerilla style I'm talking about our selling effort—an effort that focuses on building credibility and rapport, one on one with every single prospect...Guerilla style is much more of an attitude. An attitude that produces results!"

[43] Unlike intelligence, or IQ, emotional intelligence, or EQ, can be developed with practice. There are five components of emotional intelligence that will help you be more effective at creating a safe space for prospects: self-awareness, self-regulation, motivation, empathy, and social skill. The more that you can develop each of these areas, the higher your EQ. See Daniel Goldman, *Emotional Intelligence: Why It Can Matter More Than IQ*, 2005; Travis Bradberry & Jean Greaves, *Emotional Intelligence 2.0*, 2009; and Jeb Blount, *Sales EQ*, 2017.

- Fear that you'll "love them and lose them," meaning that even if they do buy, once they move into the community and become residents, future interactions with them will be very limited.

It's difficult, but your impact and success in converting higher-functioning prospects will grow if you can acknowledge and overcome your own vulnerabilities and fears heroically and with a determination to help guide the prospect, regardless of the sales result.

2. Trust the prospect.

The world of senior adults who live alone is filled with unresolved dilemmas related to driving, wellness, money, and housing.[44] Managing any of these dilemmas defies reason or logic. It requires a sustained engagement with uncertainty—marathon work with no quick fixes. As much as we would often like to "get the story" from an adult child, their emotional entanglement with childhood stories tends to increase emotional vulnerability for both the prospect and child.

Intrinsically, prospects are the only people who truly can provide meaningful responses to their own dilemmas about whether, when, and where to move. It's our job to help draw these responses out. Don't feel put off or frustrated when prospects resist, deflect, or go cold on you or their adult children. Every prospect is just trying to navigate a difficult emotional path to an important decision. Emotional resistance is a natural expression of fear and uncertainty.

Every prospect is just trying to navigate a difficult emotional path to an important decision. Emotional resistance is a natural expression of fear and uncertainty.

---

[44] While new inquiries, tours, and move-ins were down from 2019 averages, for many higher-acuity prospects, COVID-19 amplified social isolation and the difficulties of living alone. Fear generated urgency in some prospects (mostly for AL and MC) who were unable to adapt to COVID-19 by staying home. For additional detail on the impact of COVID-19 on senior living sales performance, see https://www.sherpacrm.com/2020/07/10/from-the-data-team-july covid-19-sales-performance-report/.

Acknowledge how your prospects feel, and celebrate that they trust you enough to tell you.

Sales counselors and adult children often think that they can convince, persuade, or pressure prospects into giving up decision making control. However, these tactics only succeed when there is an unavoidable crisis. To build trust and succeed at motivating self-persuasion, acknowledge and encourage a process where the prospect is in control. They are facing an emotional chasm and are the only one who will have to actually make a significant transition and bear any fallout that follows. Unless prospects agree or are in a serious health crisis, and regardless of whether you acknowledge or support it, they inevitably retain the power to veto any decision that would force them to move against their own will—and many of them do.

3. State your intentions.

During your first interaction with a prospect, state your intentions right away, and actually mean what you say. Being authentic and saying the words out loud triggers our heroic, helping selves. It helps quiet the anxiety and fear of rejection that our egos produce. It also invites trust from the prospect.

Start by explaining your role:

> "Mrs. Jones, my intention is to get to know you and to help guide you in your search, regardless of where you choose to move. Or perhaps you'll decide to stay at home. That is very much your decision."
>
> "Suzan, thank you for calling. My intention is to help guide you and your family through this decision, regardless of where your mom ultimately chooses to live."

> Be sure to acknowledge the prospect's control and autonomy: "I think that this is very much your (or your parent's) decision, and we understand that it can be emotionally wrenching."
>
> Set realistic expectations: "In our experience, there may be a series of small steps in the decision-making process. Getting ready may take some time."

4. Be fully present and actively listen.

Active listening is one of the most effective ways to establish trust, but it's hardly the easiest. When you ask a question, shut off the voice inside your head that is dying to fill the space with answers. Don't start preparing your response. Instead, be present and actually listen. Stay curious. When it's your turn to speak, acknowledge and validate what you heard, and ask follow-up questions based on what you did or did not understand. Go deep and follow the prospect's thematic content lead rather than trying to confront or persuade with solutions.

Deep down, at one time or another, all of us have had doubts and insecurities. These thoughts are amplified for higher-functioning senior living prospects since they are faced with an unwanted situation that is prompting serious consideration of a move. People are naturally more apt to trust you when you listen, truly care, and have a sincere desire to understand rather than convince them.

People are naturally more apt to trust you when you listen, truly care, and have a sincere desire to understand rather than convince them.

5. Be authentic and ditch the scripts.

Search inside of yourself for the authentic desire to get to know—and then guide—the person on the other end of the conversation. Don't worry at first if they're AL or IL. Don't ask if they're a prospect or a family member or if they're ready to tour or move in. Connect with them first, person to person. You'll be amazed at how connecting person to person builds a foundation of trust. A trusting connection will help you and your prospect have an emotionally safe space to discuss deeply personal emotional issues.

Alex and I did a review of more than 1,000 mystery shop calls to senior communities across the US during 2018. The findings showed that the average number of questions asked by sales counselors (other than typical health or financial qualifying questions) was a total of only three. Most counselors, after a couple of qualifying questions, immediately turned to prescribed, scripted statements touting the community's features and benefits.

Transcripts showed that sales counselors often spoke a lot more than they listened. Only 15 percent of sales counselors asked for the prospect's name. Fewer than 9 percent asked about problems in their current living situation. Only 3 percent asked about the prospect's life story. We assume that the overwhelming majority of the counselors we mystery shopped either didn't care enough about the prospect to ask, or they simply didn't think it was part of their sales role to ask.

> *Transcripts showed that sales counselors often spoke a lot more than they listened. Only 15 percent of sales counselors asked for the prospect's name. Fewer than 9 percent asked about problems in their current living situation. Only 3 percent asked about the prospect's life story.*

The opportunity to build trust starts from the first prospect engagement, whether it's a web inquiry, a walk-in, or a call-in. These connections can also be refreshed at various times in the sales scenario.

6. Build trust with the prospect's buying team.

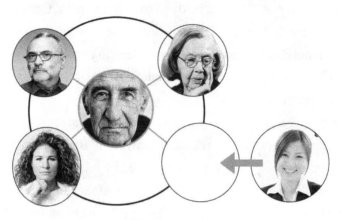

The Buying Circle

When you work in senior living, you often work with adult children and other decision influencers. For a prospect, or someone on their behalf, to inquire before a crisis almost always means they were triggered by some combination of disruptors: loneliness, isolation, physical or emotional difficulties, lack of purpose, insufficient support system, or difficulty with home maintenance. The list goes on. But often the prospect isn't the only one whose life has been disrupted, nor are they always the only person involved in decision-making.

Different members of a buying team may have different triggers, needs, perspectives, or goals. For example, a spouse or one or more adult children often bear the burdens of caregiving. They often want their parents to move but don't know how to get past their resistance, and they often feel guilty even trying.

> *To be successful, you need to understand and be able to align with each member of the buying team. One of your initial goals should be to become part of the buying team yourself.*

To be successful, you need to understand and be able to align with each member of the buying team. One of your initial goals should be to become part of the buying team yourself. At first, the prospect or another buying team member may wonder, "Why are you here?" To be accepted by the buying team, you must earn their trust and, with it, the right to ask deeply personal questions.

CASE STUDY IN TRUST BUILDING: FRANCIS

During my many turnaround campaigns, I often tried to stir up motivation in leads who had been around for a while. Essentially, my role was to cold call the cold prospects. Francis was one of those cold prospects who had inquired at the middle-class IL community we were turning around in Oklahoma.

Francis was a cheerful Dominican in his mid-80s. He was living in a three-level townhome not far from the community. The first inquiry had come in about a year before. The sales team spoke to Francis and two daughters, one of whom toured soon after. The team attempted to follow up once or twice without a response from any of them. When I first read the journal, the last attempt to connect had been over nine months ago. Seemed like a great lead to me.

After getting my own ego in check, I invoked my personal go-to hero persona, the Lone Ranger. I thought (my ego told me!) it would probably be easier to start with a call to one of his daughters, since they seemed to be urging Francis to move. But we already knew that and, but for my own fear of rejection, why not reach out directly to the decision-maker? I vowed to myself to set aside my fear of failure along with my strong urge to get another sale this month. I thought about my intentions for the conversation: be present and establish a meaningful connection.

I hoped that Francis and I would be building a conversational bridge that would lead to follow-up and advancement opportunities. There wasn't really much to plan from before the call, but I reviewed notes to consider Francis's readiness, sources of his motivators and resistance, who was already inside his buying circle, and what might help him get ready. I also did a general internet search for public information. There wasn't very much. Only then did I pick up the phone and make a call out to him.

I introduced myself: "Hi. This is David. I'm calling from Golden Pond. How are you today?" My plan was to follow Francis's lead and continue the conversational thread without trying to control or predict where it might take me. The first challenge I had was that no one on the sales team knew if Francis was male or female. The voice on the other end of the line was kind, intelligent, and somewhat high-pitched. I had a 50/50 chance and decided to take the risk of embarrassing myself, Francis, or both of us. Not far into the conversation, I got vulnerable and told Francis the truth. He laughed, thanked me for asking, and informed me that he was a man. That exchange actually broke the ice.

I learned a lot about who Francis is and was in that initial conversation. We talked for nearly an hour. Only at the very end did he ask something about available apartments. Instead, we focused on Francis. I learned that he had spent over 30 years doing scientific research at some major universities, including the University of Chicago, Berkeley, and Yale. He said his research team was trying to figure out how to get bacteria to "eat" the tail off of a viral cell. "Our success would open the door to wiping out nearly every viral disease, from the common cold to AIDS," he told me.

After acknowledging the magnitude of that effort and probing some into how his team approached the challenge, I asked Francis about whether or not he felt that they were successful. "We accomplished the result of destroying viral cells with bacteria more than once," he said. "However, we were never able to scientifically prove how to reproduce our results with clinical studies. So we never won a Nobel Prize."

Bingo. Mission accomplished; we were connected. My interest in Francis built a foundation of trust. The outcome of the conversation was a commitment to a home visit when Francis told me he really enjoyed our conversation and he wanted me to "come over and see his place."

While journaling my notes from the call, I assessed Francis's readiness. Although no longer in denial, Francis was still ambivalent about *whether* to move. When someone like Francis is stuck on *whether to move,* it's important to follow up first by acknowledging and validating their life stories. "I see you" is the takeaway that has the greatest impact.

I wanted to send Francis a personalized CFU, in part to reinforce that I could be trusted. I was hoping that my CFU might help Francis build confidence in his ability to succeed in this stage of his life. After some internet research, I found the names of some of the many articles that Francis had published. Professional. Detailed. Important stuff.

He was also somewhat of a Steady Relator, interested in how other people perceived and thought of him. Using what was by then an old version of Microsoft Publisher, I created an official-looking certificate. It had an image of a Nobel Prize medal and read, "In recognition of Francis for a lifetime dedication to scientific advancement and for being an inspiration to upcoming generations including investigation of bacteriophage tail components, phosphatases in bacteriophages, and phosphatidylinositol and ice nucleating."

I dated, signed, matted, framed, and had the certificate personally delivered to Francis on the same day as our conversation. He was blown away. He later told me, "Although my daughters were really pushing me to move, I was stubbornly holding onto my townhouse, my home. I was concerned about not fitting in or being able to make new friends. When we first spoke, I thought at last, somebody really sees me without trying to sell me anything."

Soon after, he agreed to a home visit. A week or so later, he came in for a tour. A couple of weeks after, that he came for a retour. Then he signed a lease, made his deposit, and moved in. Of all the possessions from his three-story townhouse he chose to fit into a small studio apartment, Francis found a space for the framed certificate. We truly connected!

Takeaways from Francis's Story

Looking back, every aspect of my initial encounter with Francis was a success for Francis, his daughters, our community, and my own efforts to fill the community with higher-functioning prospects. What began as an awkward retouch call to a cold lead that we knew very little about transformed into a viable interest in exploring the possibility of moving.

There were so many ways that I or another sales counselor could have derailed the chances for success with Francis, such as:

- Sending a community calendar or newsletter instead of calling.
- Calling one of his daughters first and sympathizing with her inability to get Francis to move.
- Doing a superficial "howdy doody" call to Francis but focusing on his problems and our solutions, putting the onus of taking initiative on Francis.
- Leaving the question of gender up in the air.
- Guiding the conversation to real estate and benefits.

- Failing to explore stories and details that would extend the conversation and trying to get to a yes or no decision about moving as quickly as possible.

Instead, I drew on my EQ and started by putting my own ego and fears of rejection in check. Invoking my hero and assessing my intentions helped me get outside of my own self-limiting emotions. I made myself vulnerable by admitting that I literally didn't know anything about Francis, even his gender. I focused the conversation on Francis, especially his aspirational sense of self-worth and accomplishment. This led to connection and began the process of building trust. To reinforce and advance that sense of trust, I immediately followed up with a creative, personalized gesture that communicated, "Francis, I see you."

SOME METRICS:
HOW TO TRACK CONNECTION

Tracking success with making connections and building trust creates a sales culture that builds success by valuing prospect-centered relationships. Sustaining that kind of culture requires some clear metrics.

Typically, senior living sales professionals only keep track of the tasks that a speed-to-lead sales approach uses to calculate the number of inquiries, new leads, call-ins, call-outs, tours, sales, and move-ins. There may also be brief qualitative notes that are captured, one after the other, as a date-stamped, sequential record of multiple prospect engagements. The quantitative data is compiled into sales management reports and used to calculate conversion ratios all based on the false assumption that more leads, call-outs, or tours will increase sales performance. Compiling a relevant prospect profile using common sales journaling tools was time-consuming and difficult.

Here are some key metrics that Sherpa uses to help you track how well you are connecting and building trust with any individual prospect:

What do you know?

Sometimes called discovery. The kind of discovery that I was able to learn in the initial and subsequent calls with Francis. What we learn from and about prospects is primarily a reflection of what they tell us. We can guide what prospects tell us based on the nature and content of our questions.

Connection increases and trust builds when we explore and remain curious about their life stories, especially the legacy, themes, and values behind those stories. The questioning strategy is to help the prospect self-reflect on their values and decision-making priorities. A prospect-centered journal reflects what information was drawn out through purposeful questioning. Counselors who tracked information about the prospect's life story were 30 percent more likely to close or convert that prospect than those who did not.

Impact of Journaling Discovery

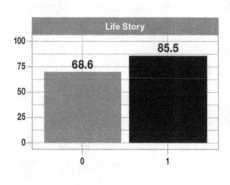
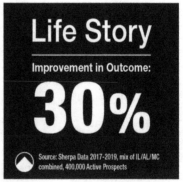

In addition to exploring their life story, identify other key areas of inquiry based on the adapted stages of readiness for change: problems in current living situation (motivators), concerns about moving now (objections), and desired features and benefits (preferences). Assess and track what information you do and don't know. Then, record additional questions relevant to filling in these content buckets.

Empathy and Connection at Work

Which community has higher conversions?

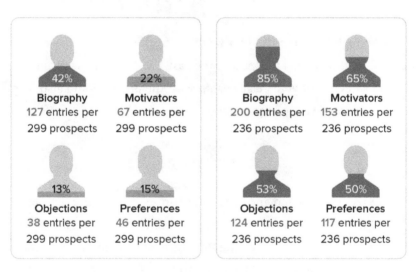

42%	**22%**	**85%**	**65%**
Biography	**Motivators**	**Biography**	**Motivators**
127 entries per	67 entries per	200 entries per	153 entries per
299 prospects	299 prospects	236 prospects	236 prospects
13%	**15%**	**53%**	**50%**
Objections	**Preferences**	**Objections**	**Preferences**
38 entries per	46 entries per	124 entries per	117 entries per
299 prospects	299 prospects	236 prospects	236 prospects

How much TSZ has been invested?

Another meaningful way to gauge the prospect's level of connection and trust is to track how much direct selling time or TSZ was invested per prospect worked, whether a new or existing lead. This can also be tracked, studied, and benchmarked by TSZ per lead worked over TSZ per counselor and per community.

What percentage of the TSZ resulted in sales activities or engagements that were initiated by the prospect?

Note that top performers, those best at building trusting relationships, have seven times as many call-ins as call-outs.

From the investment of that TSZ, how many advances were achieved?

Better connection drives more advances per prospect worked and fewer advances per move-in.

Although these metrics may be different from data you have traditionally gathered on a prospect in the past, the data points tell a meaningful story about your relationship with the prospect and also help reveal how well you are connecting.

CONCLUSION

For older adults, moving to a senior community requires letting go of the past and breaking ties to the familiar. It awakens old memories. The thought of moving naturally triggers resistance tied to fears of aging, loss of health, loss of friends, and fear of running out of money. Even if sales counselors logically overcome all apparent and stated objections related to the apartment, the pricing, or the lifestyle, higher-functioning prospects still will not move unless and until they have first confronted their fears about moving. We can help prospects like Mary and Francis confront these fears, but only after they trust that we have their best interests in mind.

The best approach to gaining their trust is to align with them in an empathic, nonjudgmental way, like we did with Mary and Francis.

Build trust and discover who they are before talking about benefits or solutions. PCS relates to the prospect in a manner that is personal, collaborative, evocative, and reflective. Before Mary and Francis were ready to hear a logical, well-reasoned set of benefits they could gain by moving, each of them had to untangle their own fears and resistance. Top senior sales performers give up control, invest the time, and ask relevant questions to connect and build trust—the kind of connection and trust needed to collaborate with the prospect through their emotional untangling process.

PCS relates to the prospect in a manner that is personal, collaborative, evocative, and reflective.

CHAPTER 6

Untangling and the Psychology of Change

"Who are you?" said the Caterpillar...
"I—I hardly know, Sir, just at Present," Alice replied rather shyly.
"At least I know who I was when I got up this morning, but I
  think I must have been changed several times since then."

—*Alice's Adventures in Wonderland*, Lewis Carroll

People are complex. As we face any major life transition, our range of emotions can tie us in knots and prevent us from making logical decisions. Our emotional core is wired in such a way that strong feelings evoke stories from our past. This is especially true for stories tied to risk, loss, or fear. For example, prospect fears about moving to any senior community might be tied to old stories about death, loss, or forcing one of their own elder family members into a poorly run, institutional SNF. The emotion behind these horror stories is strong and persistent, even if the current reality is completely different.

Conflicting perspectives, the legacy story, and the current reality often lead to ambivalence or feeling pulled in two different directions about whether to move. In these situations, using logic to persuade a prospect almost always results in pulling the emotional knot and the corresponding level of resistance even tighter. We use the term "untangling" for the psychological process that can help prospects minimize the resistance. The untangling process starts with the prospect becoming aware of an old emotional life story that builds resistance toward moving. Through advance planning and relevant questions, we can provoke, inspire, motivate, and guide the prospect through the untangling process. It's what all of our qualified but otherwise "cold" leads need from us. Untangling facilitates rational buying.

Untangling takes time. Trying to rush a prospect to decide about moving too quickly usually backfires.

Untangling takes time. Trying to rush a prospect to decide about moving too quickly usually backfires. People need time to confront and let go of or reframe feelings about their current situation in order to move forward. Our opportunity to convert higher-functioning prospects into residents lies in our willingness and ability to foster an empathic readiness to buy.

CASE STUDY: FRED AND ROSE'S AMBIVALENCE

Consider Fred and Rose, prospects for a middle-income IL community in Oklahoma. Rose was Fred's college prom sweetheart. At 83 and 78, they were still in love and had been married 50 years. Earlier, Fred had had a successful career as an insurance adjuster and had always been an adventurer. Up until a few years ago, he had spent his free time flying model airplanes and riding motorcycles.

At the point of the inquiry, however, Fred and Rose needed to change their living situation. Their two sons were concerned. Their parents' lives and relationship had changed a lot, as had their sense of personal identity. Fred was bipolar, had Alzheimer's, and had just been diagnosed with Parkinson's. He had suffered some recent falls. Rose had become his unofficial caregiver. She also took care of their 37-("and a half!")-year-old home as well as their several remaining rental properties.

Rose had just been told by her doctor that she needed to move into an AL setting because of complications from congestive heart failure. She was of slight stature, while Fred was tall and big. According to Rose, her doctor told her, "Rose, please don't try to pick Fred up when he falls. Your heart simply can't take the strain." Fred knew this and desperately wanted to avoid any risk to Rose's health. That's logical.

On the other hand, emotionally, Fred really didn't want to move. Anywhere. Ever. As a youth, his military family had forced him to move dozens of times. He had a negative association with moving, especially from a house that he and Rose had built together.

"We planned to move from here directly to [the local cemetery]," Fred said. "Some people think that moving to a retirement community is closing the casket on life. It's not. But a lot of people think that, and I would think that too."

Rationally, Fred knew he needed to move to protect Rose and himself. But he was caught up in a tangled, emotional mess. Rationally, Rose said she was ready and making plans. But emotionally, she didn't feel right acting without Fred's consent. Whenever they talked about moving, Fred would cry.

THE PUZZLE:
HOW TO UNTANGLE RESISTANCE

Higher-functioning prospects like Fred and Rose can often be ambivalent. They will get stuck with two opposite and competing arguments or positions, even when the facts surrounding a need to move are logically compelling. At The Gatesworth and other communities I worked with, I found that we could help "cold" leads like Fred and Rose untangle their emotional resistance. This is a crucial part of the decision-making process and foundational to PCS.

Our challenge in terms of teaching and training others to do what we had been doing intuitively and experientially was to develop a framework for understanding *how* people untangle. *How do they navigate change?* We needed a navigational map to identify where any prospect was on the Stages of Change continuum. To do this, we also needed a common language and set of metrics to direct the most appropriate sales activities to the right prospect at the right time.

A key to higher sales conversions is recognizing that initially, the primary sales obstacle for higher-functioning prospects, especially early on, is emotional and psychological. It's not factual, reasonable, or logical. To be able to help these prospects overcome emotional resistance to buying, we began to explore the work of Neil Rackham, a research psychologist and author of *SPIN Selling*.[45] Rackham studied sales of products that were expensive, required multiple customer interactions, and involved more than one decision-maker. While he didn't study sales with an emotional overlay, senior living seemed to meet many of the criteria he set out to study. In terms of these multi-call sales, Rackham wanted to answer a basic commonsense question: "Why do some salespeople in the same industry, selling the same products or services,

---

[45] Rackham, N. (1988). *SPIN selling*. New York: McGraw-Hill. p. 117

consistently outsell their competition?" His rigorous experimentation revolutionized how we look at the selling process.

INSIGHT FROM *SPIN SELLING*

R ackham was convinced and ultimately proved that the speed-to-lead sales approach[46] worked well for "small ticket" items that could be introduced and closed in a single customer engagement. When you're selling a product that is easy to understand, like a kitchen appliance, it's a "simple" sale. Neither the cost nor the consequences are high. There is usually only one decision-maker. It may only take one sales call, with no need for advanced planning or CFU.

There are two possible outcomes for the simple sale. Either you make a sale, or the prospect doesn't buy and becomes a "lost lead." With a small, demand-driven product, there are a large number of prospects. A speed-to-lead approach makes sense and drives quick conversions. It's a numbers game. The object is to get to yes or no quickly and then move on.

Although Rackham never specially addressed senior living sales, clearly our scenario falls into the category Rackham calls "complex" rather than simple. The cost of senior living is high. Several people are usually involved in the decision, and the prospect needs more time to decide. Perhaps most importantly, the emotional consequences of the buying decision are very high.

In a complex sale scenario, people begin the buying process at an emotional level. They feel and react to those feelings and develop an emotional predisposition long before they logically think about buying. Over time (if ever), they may confront their underlying emotions and then shift to a more logic-based process. Our challenge is to focus, invest

---

[46] First documented by Strong, E. K. (1925). Theories of selling. *Journal of Applied Psychology*, 9(1), 75-86

time, and plan next steps to build readiness within the context of this logic versus emotional ambivalence.

Our challenge is to focus, invest time, and plan next steps to build readiness within the context of this logic versus emotional ambivalence.

Rackham found that the very sales activities that worked for simple sales were counterproductive in complex, multi-call, higher-outcome sales activities. To find what did work in these scenarios, he and his team at the Huthwaite Institute evaluated 35,000 multi-call sales transcripts against 116 different factors that might affect sales effectiveness.[47]

They looked at the sales process for all kinds of large-ticket items like airplanes and mainframe computers. They focused on companies with large sales forces, such as Motorola and IBM. Rackham's research placed a great deal of emphasis on the impact of "closing" and handling objections in complex sales like senior housing. The study concluded that on average, those trained in his SPIN selling techniques had 17 percent better performance. That is impressive.

Rackham concluded that sales calls are most successful when the sales counselor is asking thought-provoking questions and the prospect is doing the talking. He found that the most successful counselors were asking specific types of open-ended questions in a specific sequence. The acronym SPIN stands for the four types of questions and the order in which they're asked:

1. **S**ituation or biographical questions are helpful for gathering and quantifying facts and data to understand the prospect's current state.

2. **P**roblem questions uncover the prospect's problems and opportunities.

---

[47] Ibid.

3. Implication questions help uncover the pain that the problem is causing or will cause.

4. Need pay-off questions task the stakeholder with finding the benefit of solving the problem, which generates self-awareness for the need to change.

Alex and I found those beliefs to be consistent with our experiences in the senior living sales trenches. More specifically, Rackham's approach to SPIN discovery and his notion of "advances" leading to closing became foundational to PCS. Our strong belief of spending more time with fewer prospects and going deep with each one was also consistent with Rackham's overall message to "slow down" discovery. Avoid being in a rush to close. Slow down the trust-building and untangling processes. Resist the urge to offer product-oriented solutions before a prospect is open and ready to make a buying decision.

In a single-call sale, the buying decision is usually made during the initial presentation with the seller present. But, says Rackham, in a multi-call sale, like those in senior living, "the most important discussions and deliberations go on when the seller isn't present, during the interval between calls."[48] An aggressive, product-centered pitch from a transactional seller usually fails because the prospect will "uncouple." They disengage or go silent purposely to avoid exposure to repeated attempts to close. Instead, slow the "getting to yes or no" process with purposeful, pre-planned questioning designed to draw out the prospect's emotional molecular core.

---

[48] Rackham, Neil (1988). *SPIN Selling.* New York: McGraw-Hill. p.117

Shortcomings of SPIN

However, we soon found that direct, ongoing application of Rackham's SPIN questioning to our senior living scenario was too difficult for industry sales professionals to understand and use day-to-day. This was in part because SPIN has a very technical orientation, with uniform, although sometimes awkward, nomenclature. These terms such, as implied versus explicit needs and type A and type B benefits were confusing, esoteric, and hard to adapt. Fred and Rose certainly had the kind of implied needs that Rackham refers to, but we needed another way to describe their situation. We needed a language and processes that were more oriented to overcoming emotional resistance.

To develop a more emotionally based senior living sales model, we turned our attention to the work of clinical and research psychologists who published extensive research on motivating change with self-persuasion in a directive way and how to measure and track the changes through discrete "stages of readiness." Their collective work was unrelated to senior living decision-making but totally consistent with Rackham's SPIN questioning techniques and sequencing. For PCS, this was our first authentic crossover that provided us with consistency in approach from these two distinct theoretical models. They were taken from different fields of study: sales and clinical psychology. Each theory was supported independently by evidence-based research and findings we could adapt to fit our own decades-long personal experiences with senior living prospects.

PERSON-CENTERED THERAPY

In the mid-1950s, Carl Rogers revolutionized what was then a more clinical counseling process. He suggested detaching the interviewing process from an authoritative, medical procedure and transformed counseling into a person-centered model. This challenged the clinical counseling approach that prevailed, characterized by a medical doctor in a white coat sitting behind a desk and examining a diagnostic checklist.

Rogers favored a different, more relaxed and empathic, and less threatening process. He believed that people could be guided to heal themselves of many psychological ailments if they were committed to speaking openly and honestly with a trained professional. The therapist established a safe and open environment for the client that became conducive to examining issues and eliciting personal reasons and methods for change.

Rather than challenging, advising, or offering solutions to the client, Rogers taught counselors to be empathic and show respect for and accept their clients and their clients' feelings. They were taught to listen rather than tell. These are all key elements in our PCS methodology.

Let's look at how focusing on empathy rather than telling might play out in senior living sales. "I'm not driving as much as I used to," a prospect tells a sales counselor. "My daughter takes me anywhere I need to go." Most counselors can't resist attacking the statement literally and with a one-size-fits-all solution: "We have a van that can also take you anywhere you need to go!"

Unfortunately, as Rackham documented, offering product-based solutions early on, like the "we have a van" response, invites objections. Offering the van is what Rackham calls a "partial solution." Offering a partial solution triggers additional concerns that then magnify the disadvantages of moving and thereby further block untangling efforts.

For example, in response to "we have a van," a prospect might respond, "Yes, of course. But my daughter drives me in my 10-year-old Buick with bucket leather seats. We love to catch up during the drives and usually listen to country music. I don't think that your van, especially when it's full of other residents, will be as comfortable or accessible as what I have now."

Offering solutions too soon keeps us from empowering the prospect to explore what Rackham calls "implied needs." In senior living, the implied need is nearly always emotional. Offering the van misses and even steers the prospect away from addressing root emotional issues. Instead, we can respond by asking legacy-oriented questions. These are open-ended and asked with an inviting and attentive body language.

Life review is an iterative and relational process. We create opportunities to empathically connect when we create a safe place for prospects to share their stories. We look for stories that uncover and clarify the values, themes, lessons, and dreams that drive them.

> We look for stories that uncover and clarify the values, themes, lessons, and dreams that drive them.

In this context, instead of talking about the van, when a prospect says something like, "I'm not driving as much as I used to," try to invite a conversation that explores driving and loss from their perspective:

- Do you remember your first car?
- What is it like for you not to be driving?
- How do you and your daughter feel about her driving you?
- What happens when your daughter isn't available?

> What they need is someone to truly care about their feelings and acknowledge, validate, and truly listen for the emotions behind the story.

Prospects don't want or need you to tell them the "right" thing to do. Few will accept or be persuaded, nor do they want you to try to solve their problems. What they need is someone to truly care about their feelings and acknowledge, validate, and truly listen for the emotions behind the story.

Rogers and his successors refined and promoted the questioning techniques that drive a client's internal motivation and confidence needed for self-persuasion. People overcame their resistance to change when the counselor acknowledged, validated, and listened for each individual person's unique perspective, feelings, and values. Unlike speed-to-lead sellers, Rogers believed that the counselor's role was to suspend judgment and create an empathic environment with unconditional positive regard. Motivation was drawn out of the client by building an awareness of the discrepancy between their legacy story, values and ideals, and current situation. Motivation to untangle that disconnect, coming from within, is what drove change.

Motivation was drawn out of the client by building an awareness of the discrepancy between their legacy story, values and ideals, and current situation. Motivation to untangle that disconnect, coming from within, is what drove change.

That is precisely the kind of questioning technique that we were looking to adapt to the senior living sales scenario.

Motivational Interviewing to Drive Change

Motivational interviewing (MI) is an extension of Rogers' model into a more directive approach. MI was developed in 2000 by William R. Miller and Stephen Rollnick, who were clinical psychologists and former students of Rogers. MI is a directive, client-centered counseling style for eliciting behavior change by helping clients to explore and resolve ambivalence. MI practitioners focus on helping people navigate and, if possible, overcome difficult habits and addictions. Like the methods studied by Rogers, it begins with making empathic connections and is collaborative, evocative, and autonomous.

However, unlike Rogers' method (and more like Rackham's), MI is aimed at achieving a particular outcome, like sobriety or ending an addiction like smoking. As we have adapted MI for PCS, the outcome is to achieve readiness in a higher-functioning senior living prospect. To achieve readiness, the counselor tries to get the prospect to confront their ambivalence or inner conflict about giving up their "home" and changing their lifestyle. The best PCS counselors learn this method while also avoiding unnecessary confrontation or uncoupling. The objective of PCS is to employ a prospect-centered, "directive method for enhancing intrinsic motivation to change (in our case to move) by exploring and resolving ambivalence."[49] MI is a proven psychological approach that facilitates overcoming emotional resistance and establishing a need or desire for many thousands of otherwise "cold" senior living prospects like Fred and Rose.

According to MI, ambivalence is "the coexistence in a person of two contradictory and incompatible emotions or attitudes, and the tension arising as a consequence."[50] This is often characterized in our sales scenario by the conflict between reason and emotion or the head and the heart. Fred expressed his ambivalence when he told us, "I don't want to move. But I just can't stay here."

When someone is struggling with two competing thoughts about a move or another big emotional decision, whichever side you focus on, promote, or argue for, pay attention to the person in conflict. They will unconsciously build arguments for the other side. Whichever side an ambivalent person supports in their own head will be the side that wins the day.

Becoming a parent teaches you about working with ambivalence. The more you try to force your teenager into doing something they absolutely should do (it's worse if you're right), the more resistance you'll encounter along the way. I've found that this can be true not only for teenagers but for coworkers, personal friends, and prospects alike.

---

[49] Miller, W. R., and S. Rollnick. *Motivational Interviewing: Preparing People for Change.* The Guilford Press, 2002.

[50] Miller, William R, and Gary S Rose. "Toward a theory of motivational interviewing." *The American psychologist* vol. 64,6 (2009): 527-37. doi:10.1037/a0016830

Senior living prospects are dealing with a loss of control at a level that is difficult for us to imagine. Their friends are dying. Their world is changing, and their bodies aren't functioning the way they used to. Their identities are often based on careers they or their spouses no longer have. Our higher-functioning prospects are naturally resistant to any further loss of control or anything they perceive as the beginning of the end. If you as a trusted counselor try to offer solutions that seem to minimize their very real fears, frustrations, and sadness, you'll be met with resistance. The resistance is emotional and is most often expressed as, "I'm not ready yet."

Over the years, I've seen situations where prospects have been over-powered and forced to make a decision, either by an overly aggressive salesperson or a well-meaning adult child. Those prospects typically move into your community but are unhappy and complain endlessly about the services. They were never given the opportunity to resolve their resistance. They weren't given the basic freedom to *choose* to act in their own best interest. We can and should do better.

Applying MI: Going with the Skid

After connecting and building trust, we guide and support the prospect with open-ended questions. These questions spark reflection and elicit stories that help build awareness in the mind of the prospect.[51] When they tell these stories, prospects hear themselves talk about the key themes and values that they built their lives around. They are themes and values like independence, self-reliance, courage, creativity, staying engaged and productive, exploring new activities, romance, etc. These are nearly always at odds with their current living situation and decision

---

[51] The most helpful questions for senior living prospects who are still ambivalent about moving anywhere (those in denial or thinking stages) relate to the prospect's personal life story or "legacy," as described in *How to Say It to Seniors* (Solie, 2004), p. 35-46.

One way we can help prospects untangle ambivalence about moving is by what I call "going with the skid." By this, I mean that rather than challenging the premise, you can instead accept it and then steer the conversation toward the source of resistance.

to stay. When a prospect becomes aware of this discrepancy, they are motivated to get ready for a change.

One way we can help prospects untangle ambivalence about moving is by what I call "going with the skid." By this, I mean that rather than challenging the premise, you can instead accept it and then steer the conversation toward the source of resistance.[52] It's the polar opposite to most transactional sales training that teaches us to stay in control, extract product-related needs, and then value-match solutions against those needs.

Let's go back to Fred and Rose for a brief example of what a conversation might sound like between a sales counselor employing MI and someone like Fred who is struggling with *whether* to move. Intellectually, Fred knows he should move. It's logical. Yet his emotions strongly resist letting go.

Here's an example of a conversation where the senior living sales counselor goes with the skid:

> Counselor: My goodness, this must be hard for you. I know that Fred has been forced to move so many times during his life and finally feels settled here. I can't begin to imagine how much you treasure the memories you created with your family in this home. And your garden! How many hours have you spent taking care of it over the years? Let me ask you: are you sure you can't stay here?
>
> Fred: Yes, it is very difficult. We built this home and planned to

---

[52] The MI theory describes this technique as "rolling with resistance." One view of resistance is that the client is behaving defiantly. Another viewpoint is that resistance is a signal that the client views the situation differently. This requires you to understand your client's perspective. Resistance is a signal to you to change direction or listen more carefully. Miller and colleagues have identified and provided examples of at least seven ways to react appropriately to client resistance (Miller and Rollnick, 1991).

stay here till death. It's like we planned to bake a cake, and now it's nothing but mush.

A bit later in the conversation, the counselor pivots from going with the skid to summarizing and reinforcing Fred's own statements that push against his resistance. In other words, they support Fred's attempts at self-persuasion or change talk:

> Counselor: So as I understand your concerns, in order to avoid becoming more dependent on your children, you have started looking at some senior living communities like ours. You have shared with me how many times you were forced to move growing up and that you built this house so you would never have to move again. It must have taken a lot of courage for you to start looking. How do you feel about your options?
>
> Fred: Yes, that's right. How do I feel? Well, I get a little angry when I ask myself, "Well, what the hell are you gonna do about it?" Sometimes I feel like I have become so damn feeble.
>
> Counselor: It sounds like your current living situation is making things very sad for you. How would you like to see things be different?

The counselor is now inviting Fred to suggest the basis for moving, for a change.

> Fred: I just don't know. It's so damn frustrating. I really don't want to move, but with Rose's heart problems, I can't continue to live here either. Honestly, we feel like we are in limbo.
>
> Counselor: Sounds like you don't have very good choices.
>
> Fred: I don't think so. No, I don't.

By making a simple acknowledgment of a prospect's very real fears, sorrows, and unresolved ambivalence, the counselor creates awareness and an opportunity for empathic connection. This is trust-building.

When they become more aware of the reality of their concerns, Fred and Rose start to openly acknowledge some of their problems.

> Rose: Oh yes, we spent the happiest years of our life in this house. And when properly attended to, our garden is lovely. But you know what the doctor and our children are saying. Caregiving for Fred is becoming more and more difficult.
>
> Fred: Yeah. It's just not the same, and Rose is getting worn out taking care of all of it alone.

At this point, an experienced sales professional may feel the urge to pivot, pounce, and begin selling the idea of moving as a solution. But our effectiveness in untangling will significantly increase if instead of offering solutions just yet, we slow down, probe, and explore a little further the option of them just staying home. Again, go with the skid:

> Counselor: Have you thought about hiring someone to help Rose with the housekeeping and caregiving duties, even someone to take over the rental properties so you can stay here a while longer? Would that help?

Openly acknowledge that staying home is an option. Actually, it is the option that they are choosing when they don't accept change. Validating and reinforcing that staying home is the default result of doing nothing helps create a mutual understanding of what it would mean for Fred and Rose to leave their home. With this conversational approach, we are assisting them internally to increase awareness of and motivation to confront their own ambivalence. It provokes, inspires, and motivates them to state their opposition to staying. That's untangling and moves prospects closer to a rational decision about whether to stay or move. But take your time. Untangling happens only after multiple engagements and a number of false starts.

People, including our prospects, don't want to be told what the "right" thing is for them to do. They don't want others to try to solve their problems for them. This is why very few higher-functioning prospects ever choose to move into our communities. And this is why going with the skid of prospect resistance will propel

> People, including our prospects, don't want to be told what the "right" thing is for them to do. They don't want others to try to solve their problems for them.

both you and the prospect forward on a journey of navigating change. This is selling with a prospect-centered approach.

SLOW DOWN THE SELLING PROCESS

For Fred, the emotional resistance might be: "I am afraid that I have lost my role as the family provider and become a burden to Rose. I feel helpless and emasculated." For Rose, resistance may stem from a fear of no longer being capable of being a "good wife and support system for Fred." Emotional resistance is usually grounded in stories from past experiences that keep prospects from being aware or accepting of their subconscious, often desperate need for change. We can help if only we can stop

> Emotional resistance is usually grounded in stories from past experiences that keep prospects from being aware or accepting of their subconscious, often desperate need for change.

trying to "sell" before we help prospects accept the need for change and explore and confront their underlying emotions.

Until there are clear signs that the prospect is psychologically ready to move, questions also need to address problems and difficulties in the current living situation as well as the implications and consequences of those problems, just as Rackham demonstrated.[53] However, for the

---

[53] It appears that until there are clear signs that the prospect is ready to move somewhere, questions also need to address problems and difficulties in the current living situation as well as the implications and consequences of those problems (Rackham, 1988).

Slowing down the selling process and investing the time needed to connect and untangle before trying to persuade or convince using product-oriented benefits is what produces better conversion results.

prospect to even be willing to discuss these very personal questions, PCS encourages the sales counselor to first connect by building trust. As Rogers and MI demonstrate, this results in a working relationship that aligns and collaborates with the prospect. It provides an empathic connection that invites and provokes the prospect to confront emotional barriers. Slowing down the selling process and investing the time needed to connect and untangle before trying to persuade or convince using product-oriented benefits is what produces better conversion results.

Empathic connections open up the possibility for emotional untangling. Motivation for change fuels the untangling process. Purposeful questioning, beginning with life stories, enhances motivation. All of this warming up takes time, patience, and empathic concern from the counselor. Investing time to connect and listen to life stories, as well as engaging in wandering and repeated conversations, often reveals important themes and provides meaningful clues both to the sales counselor and to the prospect themselves. You both can start to define and understand the prospect's legacy, motivations, and resistance. Unlike trying to meet quotas for sales tasks and activities, exploring life stories can also help generate achievement drive, activation energy, and excitement for members of the sales team.

CONCLUSION: KEYS TO UNTANGLING

Overall, the untangling process with prospects and their adult children is a lot like talking to a close friend or confidant about a deeply personal dilemma. Once prospects like Fred and Rose trust you and your intentions and know that you are present and genuinely interested in their responses beyond framing what you might say next, the rest will follow naturally. "In the end, it is not about getting them to move but instead helping them to get ready [emotionally] to break camp [when they decide it's time]. It is about assisting them in preserving the ultimate independence, control, and gratitude for one more 'good' day while it lasts," says Solie.[54]

Giving up the result, such as a tour or sale, is the hard part for most sales counselors. It's counterintuitive. But when we as sales counselors try to tell someone what they *should* do, or when we try to control the outcome, prospects who are emotionally ambivalent often respond by doing the opposite. Why doesn't speed-to-lead selling work in senior living? Because if someone is predisposed to say no, then presenting a yes-or-no question by quickly selling well-meaning solutions will simply get you to a no sooner.

If senior living sales were a foot race, most senior living operators would run marketing marathons and sales sprints. These are long, continuous, never-ending lead generation campaigns that continue regardless of how many leads they already have or how many they reasonably can work with. That's the volume part.

Once a prospect is deemed to be "sales qualified," transactional sellers rush to qualify, get in for a tour, and then attempt to close with product-specific, needs-matching closing techniques. But untangling deep-seated emotions takes multiple attempts. Done properly, the PCS conversion process is more like running a sales marathon than a sprint.

> Done properly, the PCS conversion process is more like running a sales marathon than a sprint.

The basic premise that distinguishes our sales approach from a speed-to-lead approach is our core belief that we can help otherwise cold

---

[54] Solie, D., *Home Rules: We're Not Going Anywhere,* https://www.davidsolie.com/blog/home-rules-were-not-going-anywhere.

prospects get ready. Untangling takes place, if at all, inside the prospect's own thoughts and feelings. The power of PCS lies in motivating and guiding the prospect in talking about their resistance openly to us as an empathic listener. They can trust us and share thoughts about their journey through the untangling or getting-ready process. Small advances can be observed in distinct actionable stages that we can identify, work with, and even build a sales pipeline around.

CHAPTER 7

Advancing Toward "Ready"

The great majority of people are "wandering generalities" rather than "meaningful specifics." The fact is that you can't hit a target that you can't see. If you don't know where you are going, you will probably end up somewhere else. You have to have goals.

—Zig Ziglar

It's time to redefine what we think day-to-day "success" means in senior living sales. Time to clarify the intended target of our efforts. To fully succeed, we shouldn't try to connect and untangle resistance with our prospects solely for the sake of building relationships. While that may be a useful cause, our primary outcome, and that of our operators and investors, should be for us to convert more prospects into residents faster. Top sales performers who use PCS don't make an either-or choice between an emotional connection and a sales outcome. A successful sales effort with qualified, higher-functioning prospects should lead to more emotional connections, more untangling resistance, *and* more prospects who buy.

For many operators using a transactional, speed-to-lead method (including me early on), there are only a very limited set of milestones to evaluate sales performance. How many new prospects inquired? Of those who did inquire, how many came in for at least one tour? Of the qualified new inquiries who toured, how many moved in? Not many options or short-term outcomes to target if you get stuck along the way.

Alex and I wanted to refine our successful personal experiences in the community turnaround leasing trenches and create a practical, sustainable, and scalable methodology that included short-term outcomes for counselors to target. We all want to see our communities full of happy, higher-functioning residents. But sales success doesn't occur from the first call, when the prospect does an on-site tour, or even when a contract is signed. For senior living sales, where both cost and emotional resistance are high, success comes from helping a prospect advance in lots of small steps over time.

As we help an individual prospect get ready to buy, how do we assess and plan for the many and varied steps needed to reach that pivot point? When do we get to a place where the prospect is freed of emotional resistance and ready to make a logical buying decision?

STAGES OF READINESS FOR CHANGE MODEL

To help us better understand how to allocate our limited sales resources, we adapted an evidence-based theoretical model to get better tour-to-move-in ratios. The Transtheoretical or Stages of Change model, developed by clinical psychologist James Prochaska, et al., helped fill in the gap in PCS. Regardless of the lifestyle behavior being confronted, Prochaska found that people experience and advance through changing behavior in one of six stages of readiness. He also found that as people go through these stages, they experience a distinct series of emotions and behaviors that can be mapped by stage and along a predictable continuum of readiness.

Stages replace the ambiguous and urgency-based sales milestones of hot, warm, and cold that are commonly used. Instead, the Stages of Change model identifies behaviors and statements that are typical of each stage. It gives sales counselors an over-view of purposeful and targeted open-ended questioning, planning, and CFU strategies. These stages plot out a navigational map of the readiness journey of a higher-functioning prospect, akin to the journey of anyone con-sidering a significant lifestyle change, regard-less of what kind of change is being considered. Similar to the Kübler-Ross model for the

Stages replace the ambig-uous and urgency-based sales milestones of hot, warm, and cold that are commonly used. Instead, the Stages of Change model identifies behaviors and statements that are typical of each stage.

stages of grief (denial, anger, bargaining, depression, acceptance), the behaviors associated with each stage are baked into the human psyche.

The Stages of Change model is a framework for understanding the process of incremental behavior change. Of the six stages of readiness for change identified by Prochaska, we found four to be most useful and adaptable for use in the senior living sales scenario. We named the four stages denial, thinking, planning, and action. At any time during the senior living sales process, the things each prospect does and says are associated with one of the four stages of readiness.

The Stages of Change model is a framework for understanding the process of incremental behavior change.

As with any dramatic lifestyle change, there are actually two decisions a person needs to make rather than one. Think of it as a two-step dance where the prospect leads. The first step or decision point is *whether* to stay based on perceived pros and cons. Unless a prospect believes that the advantages of moving outweigh the disadvantages of staying, they never reach or pivot to consideration of the second decision.

During the sales process, each senior living prospect's behavior and statements can be associated with one of four identifiable stages of read-iness. No one stage is considered to be more important than another. Linear progression through each of the stages is possible, but we've found it to be very rare. Depending on what triggers the initial inquiry, prospects can start out at any one of the four stages. In general, the more crisis driven and higher acuity the prospect is, the more likely they will be ready to move at the time of inquiry. Prospects (and their adult children) can also move either toward or away from readiness.

Denial Stage

In the first stage of readiness, senior living prospects are most clearly not ready to make any decision, especially not one to buy. Only about 5 percent of your prospects will be in the denial stage. Prospects who are in denial may say something like, "I will *never* make a move from my home. Ever!" Someone clearly inquired on their behalf, but the prospect is making (or taking charge of not making) the decision.

At the denial stage, prospects:

- Minimize unpleasant occurrences and pretend that disagreeable realities don't exist.
- Are not fully aware or accepting of the consequences of staying home.
- Are defensive and often deflect, discount, or deny conversations about problems and difficulties in their current situation.
- Often rationalize with quasi-logical explanations for staying or intellectualize using abstract analysis to rob events of personal significance.
- Are often in your lead base due to the initiative of an adult child, family member, or professional influencer such as a trust officer, eldercare attorney, case manager, etc.

For example, during our sales engagement with Fred and Rose, Fred started out in denial. Rose made the initial inquiry. Here's an excerpt from one of our initial conversations:

Counselor: How did you start the process of looking at assisted living communities?

Rose: Our doctors told us we had no choice and would have to move to an assisted living community. So I called some places.

Fred (in denial): I don't really believe what the doctor said. I'm going to see another doctor.

Counselor: Maybe you're hoping that someone says they were wrong the whole time?

Fred: That's right. I wish that they would look into it and see that it was all a mistake.

The strategic readiness advance for someone in denial is to help prospects think about the possibility of making a lifestyle change. For example, this could mean moving out of their current residence without regard to when or where they may move sometime in the future.

Thinking Stage

Prospects in this stage have become ambivalent about *whether* they should make a move or consider a change. About 60 percent of the typical senior living lead base inquire when they are in the thinking stage. In terms of increasing conversions, the thinking stage has the greatest opportunity.

Compared to those in denial, prospects in the thinking stage are:

- Less defensive and willing to explore problems and difficulties in their current residence.
- Aware and accepting of the difficulties that create ambivalence, which gives sales counselors something to work with using MI.
- Ambivalent about *whether* to stay in or leave their current residence.

- Aware of a growing discrepancy between the reality of how they are living contrasted with their values and aspirational self-image.
- Fearful about letting go of the nostalgic sense of security, comfort, and familiarity of the status quo.

The prospect's feelings most associated with the thinking stage are sadness and anger. They are emotionally focused on holding on or looking back, longing for "how things used to be." Thinkers are holding on to old stories, deep-seated memories, and the emotions that are tied into what they have long seen as "home."

The strategic goal for interacting with prospects in the thinking stage is to evoke "pro-change talk." In these discussions, the prospect is questioned, provoked, and guided to openly acknowledge, out loud, the problems and disadvantages that they see in their current situation. Sales counselors should start with open-ended questions that can intensify or amplify the discrepancies between their prospect's goals, values, and themes (drawn from life stories) and the reality of their current living situation.

A word of caution to sales counselors: don't offer product-based solutions to prospects in the thinking stage. As a trusted counselor, you should go slow and try to explore feelings instead of having fast and shallow conversations about the product. Motivating change is an inside-out, evocative process. Ask more direct questions to clarify and elaborate on each of your prospect's problems, and go with the skid to address ambivalence.

Motivating change is an inside-out, evocative process.

For prospects in the thinking stage, you can mirror and clarify their responses. Summarize what they've said, and reflect on the emotions surrounding their statements. If you're unsure of what lies behind a statement, form a reasonable guess as to what they meant, and then give their words a new voice in the form of validation and acceptance. These statements should check, rather than assume, that what you've heard is correct. This technique can help you explore discrepancies between what the prospect is saying and how they really feel.

Fred: When you get to this point, life just isn't what you thought. It's kind of like going and getting the cake and it's nothing but mush. But you've got to finally decide that you're not going to live forever. Someday you're going to have to close the casket.

Counselor: Wow, that's very interesting. What you are saying is that many people feel that a move to assisted living is closing the casket. Do you think that's true?

Fred: Well, I don't think it's true. But some people may think it is. And I might think that sometimes, too.

For a prospect and their family members, advancing from thinking to planning requires a leap of faith. They are taking a big risk by accepting and agreeing to the need to make a move. At the same time, they are being challenged to let go of all that was, including their home, identity, memories, and sense of familiarity with the world around them. Moreover, imagine being in a prospect's shoes, courageously and hopefully accepting that you can't continue with the way things have been. Then what?

Planning Stage

About 30 percent of the typical senior living leads are in the planning stage, which follows thinking. Moving into planning, prospects have bravely resolved their ambivalence about *whether* to make a change. They have accepted that there is no going back to the way things used to be. This is where life gets really scary.

William Bridges describes this stage in the decision-making context as the "neutral zone" where one is in "no man's land."[55] Brené Brown describes it as "that middle space when you're in the dark—the door has closed behind you. You are too far in to turn around and not close enough to the end to see the light."[56]

In the early planning stage, prospects are straddling the tension that lies between wanting their lives to go back to the way things were and being pulled forward into an unknown, uncomfortable, and unwelcomed new reality. This is the pivot point in the prospect's emotional and decision-making journey.

Planners:

- Openly acknowledge the problems and difficulties of staying home.
- Are driven by the prevailing emotion that is a fear of the unknown. Now the issue shifts to a consideration about *when* to change their living situation, not *whether*. Similar to when we might decide to go on a diet, prospects in this stage are comfortable with their current eating habits and a bit fearful of the new behaviors related to dieting. In the planning stage, we know we have to lose weight, but we become focused on, "Just how long can I delay getting started?"

A good start for the planning stage is to summarize a prospect's current situation as you have come to understand it. For example:

Counselor: Rose, as I understand it, you really like your home. You and Fred built it. Your memories are here. You planned to die

---

[55] William Bridges, *The Way of Transition*, embracing life's most difficult moments, Da Capo Press, 2001, p. 155. "The neutral zone is the in-between time, after you have given up your old identity but before you have fully discovered your new one...it's a colorless streak of emptiness that spreads across your life, like the gray smear left by a dirty eraser."

[56] Brené Brown, *Rising Strong*, 2015. P 27.

here. Fred wants to stay here a while longer. On the other hand, your children and your doctor have told you that it is not safe for you to stay here and take care of the house and yard and manage your rental properties. It's just too much. Fred alone is a full-time job. Is that a fair summary? How do you see your options?

Often prospects in the planning stage will ask for advice. That is the situation that Rose is in. She openly acknowledges that they need to move. Up until this point, our most effective role has been to support and probe awareness of emotional resistance.

Beginning in the planning stage, the sales counselor's role shifts to more of a trusted guide. In this role, we provided Rose information to help her explore options and formulate a "change plan." We asked, "How would you like for things to be different?" As with every prospect engagement, we tried to get a commitment, even for something small like another visit to further explore what the future could be like. You can also offer your assistance with resources to help with downsizing or developing a moving plan. Invite them to participate in your community and experience a program, a meal, or even a trial stay.

Action Stage

In the final stage of readiness, prospects are committed to making a move in the near future. They are simply deciding *where* to move. While only about 5 to 10 percent of prospects are actually in the action stage at the time of inquiry, most senior living operators treat all new prospects as if they arrive "ready" to buy. However and whenever a prospect arrives in the action stage, our role as sellers shifts to a more traditional solution- or benefits-based orientation. The action stage is where counselors need to overcome obstacles and become practical problem-solvers.

The strategic goal in the action stage is to get a move-in commitment, an initial deposit, and a targeted move-in date. This is the time to "sell" in a more traditional and transactional sense:

- Engage in active discussion and education about senior living and what's different and better about your community as compared to what they would experience if they were to move to a competitive senior community.
- Match specific benefits in your community's amenities, programs, and service offerings to your prospect's individual needs, desires, and preferences.
- Describe your community's leasing process and details, and discuss setting a specific move-in date.
- Solicit support and encouragement from the prospect's family members and their social support system.

> The action stage is much different from the denial and thinking stages, when we encourage sales counselors to first and foremost connect empathically and build trusting relationships.

The action stage is much different from the denial and thinking stages, when we encourage sales counselors to first and foremost connect empathically and build trusting relationships. Product differentiation and value-matching, while counterproductive in early stages, are very important for prospects in the later planning and action stages.[57] We think of this as the second step of a two-step dance. You need to wait for your cue for the elusive pivot point in the prospect's decision-making process. In my experience, the cue to pivot always comes from the prospect. You know you're at the pivot point when prospects begin to turn the conversation

---

[57] Miller and Rollnick (1991, p. 203) have called this "Phase 2 of Motivational Interviewing." The counselor's job changes "from one of motivating change to a more action-oriented role." This is when Prospect-Centered Selling most clearly resembles transactional selling. In the action stage, the counselor's focus shifts from untangling emotions to gaining a commitment for the sale.

to an examination of the sales process or solution options. Then the counselor's job changes from one of gently motivating change to a more action-oriented role. Again, follow the prospect's lead. If they have a desire to move and a reasonable time frame, it's time to employ your most effective sales closing strategies!

Stages of Readiness

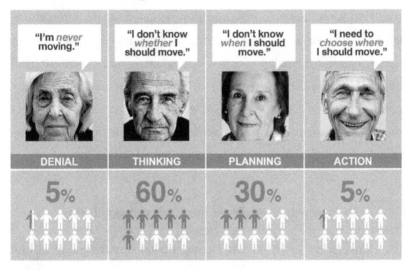

"I'm *never* moving."	"I don't know *whether* I should move."	"I don't know *when* I should move."	"I need to *choose where* I should move."
DENIAL	**THINKING**	**PLANNING**	**ACTION**
5%	60%	30%	5%

STEP-BY-STEP ADVANCES

With the stages of readiness for change model in mind, we can develop new metrics for success. If we only celebrate closings, the sales team suffers from having only about five events per month to celebrate. It's discouraging. Just counting sales and lost lead outcomes is also not an effective way to gauge, predict, or enhance day-to-day sales performance. It also won't actually help the higher-functioning prospects to make a positive change in their lives.

The adapted readiness for change model offers a different and better way to track, classify, and prioritize the active lead base. It also empowers and intrinsically motivates your sales counselors. More importantly, it facilitates a process that helps prospects and their key influencers address and overcome deep-seated emotional barriers to change.

> The adapted readiness for change model offers a different and better way to track, classify, and prioritize the active lead base.

The overwhelming number of sales engagements (whether in senior living or elsewhere) results in what Rackham calls a continuation—namely, "interactions where there is no commitment or progress toward a buying decision by the prospect."[58] A small percentage of total interactions do result in an advance (versus a continuation). In a higher-performing senior living community, this could be as many as 50 to 60 prospect advances per month. Understanding what an advance is and how to generate more of them is key to increasing sales conversion rates.

1. Advancing readiness in a series of small steps.

Each advance is a small success. Each one takes time, preparation, and follow-up. Rackham says advances occur "when an event that takes place, either during a call or visit or just after it, that moves the sale forward toward a decision...by understanding what kind of advance would be required to make a call or visit successful, top salespeople set...objectives [engagement targets] that move sales forward."[59]

> Each advance is a small success. Each one takes time, preparation, and follow-up.

The most successful sales counselors, according to Rackham, are those who can convert continuations into advances. Advances in the

---

[58] Rackham, N., *SPIN Selling*, McGraw-Hill Book Company, New York, 1988. P. 44-46
[59] Ibid.

early stages of change are the sales equivalent of getting on base in baseball. Each small prospect advance sets up additional opportunities for closes later in the selling process. Advances, like baseball's walks, singles, and doubles, don't actually score runs. However, these are the small steps that put more players into a position where they can score.

> *Advances, like baseball's walks, singles, and doubles, don't actually score runs. However, these are the small steps that put more players into a position where they can score.*

Drawing from the psychology of change, an advance in the senior living sales scenario occurs when something happens that demonstrates that the prospect is moving toward ready in the Stages of Change continuum. They advance when they are more ready, emotionally, to begin to evaluate possibilities and options rationally and logically. This "something" could be changes in health, living situation, support system, or some other life-impacting event.

Advances could also come from us purposefully and regularly engaging with prospects during home visits and personalized CFU (see Chapter 6). Whatever the "something" is, the prospect has a new awareness and/or stronger motivation to logically confront problems in their current living situation. This kind of advance motivates higher-functioning prospects to confront their ambivalence and do something toward making a change. This kind of advance is a meaningful result for sales counselors to target.

Keep in mind each advance represents a commitment on the part of the prospect. Advances beget more advances. Why? According to psychology expert Robert Cialdini, "Once we have committed to an idea or goal, we are strongly motivated to honor that commitment to remain

> *"Once a prospect agrees to take a step forward, they experience a drive to take additional steps in that direction."*

consistent. Once a prospect agrees to take a step forward, they experience a drive to take additional steps in that direction."[60]

2. What is an advance in senior living sales?

Advances are like aiming for a walk or a base hit and not trying to always hit a home run.

Think of each advance as a small but significant "close."

Advances are like aiming for a walk or a base hit and not trying to always hit a home run. Deposits, leases, and move-ins in senior living communities are often the result of many hours of hard work.

Small commitments, ones that require the prospect either to demonstrate a higher level of trust in us or agree to something new, are advances. Think of each advance as a small but significant "close." In general, we identified three areas where advances can happen:

- **Time:** When prospects or their decision influencers agree to meet with us or schedule a phone call, that commitment to engage time is an advance.
- **Emotional engagement:** A prospect connects with us and then answers personal, emotionally charged questions. They actively participate in direct conversations about their current and desired situations. When there is trust, prospects lower their emotional barriers and share personal information, life stories, or even some long-kept secret that reveals a vulnerable confidence. It is an advance if they invite or permit us to speak to their adult children. These are all emotional engagements that result in an advance in the readiness for change and eventually a logical buying decision.

---

[60] *Influence: Science and Practice*, 2001 (4th Edition) Allyn & Bacon. For more on *Why Advances Work*, see James Muir, http://www.puremuir.com/leverage-hidden-science-behind-advancing-sale/.

- **Commitment:** When prospects share personal financial information, make introductions to important decision influencers, agree to take tours, allow a home visit, or follow up, it is an advance. It's also an advance when they commit to seriously consider our community as a place to live, make a deposit, or sign a contract.

Small, incremental advances are possible multiple times every day and with most of our qualified prospects, even the "cold" leads. Again, looking at on-base percentages in baseball, striving for advances with any particular prospect may or may not result in a sale. But selling to seniors, like baseball, "is a game of probabilities and you could shift the probabilities slightly, but not perfectly, in your favor. Individual [results] are a crapshoot; luck rules, bad luck kills, and individual performances can overcome all other factors."[61] Measuring and tracking each of these various types of advances provides us an ongoing, granular, and relevant view of sales effectiveness.

The critical fact is that a consistent focus on advances with higher-functioning prospects adds up. Over time, it is more advances rather than more inquiries or more tours that naturally produces more sales. That's why we should celebrate every advance as a success, even if it doesn't directly result in an immediate sale.

STRATEGIC ADVANCES BASED ON STAGES OF READINESS

The overarching strategy of PCS is that our sales professionals can guide higher-functioning prospects toward getting ready. And this opens up the possibility of converting substantially more prospects. By

---

making empathic connections, untangling emotional resistance, and then making a strategic advance, we get to the point where the prospect is ready to make a logical decision about when and where to move.

Readiness advances can and do occur at every stage of the prospect's buying journey. Using the idea of a four-quadrant readiness grid, we now have a language to describe where someone is on the readiness for change continuum. We also know what kind of questioning, CFU, and engagement to focus on. The Stages of Change guide us on how to strategically assess what we think it might take not to close but to advance a prospect's readiness based on their current stage. Assess, prescribe, choose a tactic, and then execute. As the prospect's emotional state may well be in flux, consider this assessment to be ongoing, iterative, and dynamic.

We can make an initial readiness assessment based on the prospect's statements. These statements are grouped based first on whether they are feeling positive or negative about staying and then whether they are pro or con when it comes to moving. To help sort these stages out, think about a significant life change that you have personally experienced.

For example, consider the emotional journey that accompanies a romantic breakup. As we first notice signs of relationship strain, we are often in denial, focusing instead on the advantages of staying in the relationship. There comes a time when we are aware of the disadvantages of staying in the relationship and may even openly talk about wishing things could be like they used to be. We are thinking about the pros and cons of staying versus leaving. Only after we conclude that it's better to leave than stay do we begin to plan when and then choose what comes next. Along with grief and other types of loss, there is a predictable pattern of the emotions we feel at various discrete stages. Just as it takes time for us to process these emotions, it also takes time for your prospect to accept their own significant life change.

After you identify the pro or con of key prospect statements, identify your prospect's current readiness stage: denial, thinking, planning, or action. Wherever you assess them in terms of readiness, your strategy for advancing will always be to help the prospect get to the next stage in the readiness continuum. For example, this could be from denial to thinking, thinking to planning, planning to action, or action to move-in.

On a foundational level, your readiness advancement strategy is associated with which Stages of Change the prospect is starting from. This model is like the compass rose that helps us talk about, plan from, and choose questions to address each stage of readiness. Consider the following guidelines:

Table 2: Guidelines for Advancing Prospects Through the Stage of Change Continuum.

Stage of Change	The next strategic advance occurs when the prospect is:	Actions to Help Prospect Advance
Stage 1: Denial Stuck and hoping for magic	Thinking about problems and difficulties in current residence.	Align, build trust, and validate feelings. Acknowledge their control of the decision. Explore expected outcomes of staying home without expressing judgment. Evoke life stories and listen for themes and values.

Stage 2: Thinking Thinking about problems and difficulties; on the fence about *whether* to move or stay	Willing to acknowledge problems and explore solutions.	Promote self-confidence by evoking stories about prior life changes that were successful. Promote self-evaluation of staying at home through use of reflections, statements that amplify the prospect's perceived difficulties, and pro and con position summaries. As trust is built, ask more direct questions and probe their perceptions of each problem area.
Stage 3: Planning Testing the waters. The issue is *when* to move, now or later	Open to considering the benefits of making a change, including a move to senior housing.	Clarify prospect goals. Summarize the situation and elicit what solutions they are considering; offer to help resolve stated financial or logistical obstacles, whether that involves a move to your community or not. Suggest options and encourage small steps. Solicit collaboration with family/friends.
Stage 4: Action Choosing *where* to move among competing senior communities	Ready to make a commitment, hopefully to move into your community	Praise the decision to move somewhere, anywhere. Provide information about your product/service package. Value-match prospect needs to what your community offers. Ask for a commitment and offer assistance to address any perceived barriers.

The Stages of Change model provides action-oriented guidelines that motivate and inspire heroic senior living sales professionals to engage in meaningful and proactive outreach particularly for higher-functioning or "cold" leads. The table above displays some considerations that characterize each of the stages. Your best strategy will evolve as untangled prospect emotions reveal themselves through life stories and trust breakthroughs. These stories will expose important life themes and values. You can follow them with reflections and summations that repeat what you heard—without judgment.

The content and intentions behind your open-ended questions, at any stage, are grounded in your strategy. You can employ a variety of tactics to execute and deliver your plan: call-out, email-out, Skype, Zoom, home visits, event invitations, a meaningful CFU, or an on-site tour. From time to time, you may need to reassess. You may need to adjust your tactics. Your heroic strengths are curiosity, an empathic heart, courage, and determination. Investing the time to create a personalized readiness plan for next steps will often help you generate additional advances.

Your heroic strengths are curiosity, an empathic heart, courage, and determination.

CHAPTER 8

Purposeful, Proactive Planning for Next Steps

I have always found that plans are useless, but planning is indispensable!

—Dwight D. Eisenhower

E ffective planning is focused and deliberate. As a lawyer, I spent a great deal of time building case studies to better understand any subject matter relevant to my client's situation. I researched relevant legislation and case law. I identified the underlying issues and then planned my strategy carefully. In sales, I realized that our

Effective planning is focused and deliberate.

industry does not typically consider the time invested in *planning how to gain an advance during a conversation* as a "selling" activity. Yet, it is just as valuable to converting prospects as time spent *actually engaged in a conversation*. The more prepared my sales teams and I are, the more likely we are to get advances with prospects.

It turns out that the most successful approach to senior living planning is similar to legal planning in that it needs to be thoughtful, compassionate, purposeful, and *actionable*. If a specific plan isn't working, the best-performing senior living counselors remain agile and open to making modifications. If we believe that a prospect would have a better quality of life by moving, then a determination is critical to achieving success. Think of the process as a relentless pursuit to evoke a logical buying decision. If a tactic fails or even backfires, we try another one.

PCS strives first to build trust and seek discovery to properly assess the prospect's situation, especially in terms of their Stage of Change In turn, the assessment provides a navigational road map to develop meaningful strategies for our questioning, conversations, follow-up, and engagements.

In practice, PCS planning is designed to proactively create next steps that will increase the probability of advancing readiness. The most impactful next steps are meaningful and personalized rather than mechanical. PCS plans are personalized, one size fits one. An effective PCS plan is one that iteratively assesses how to advance across the readiness gap with a series of small steps. Prospects move one step at a time, whether any particular advance results in an imminent sale or not. Success is similarly gauged on the prospect's personal journey across the readiness continuum.

PCS planning for individual prospect case studies is different than a transactional or speed-to-lead-oriented sales planning process in a number of ways, including:

- PCS planning is a collaborative, empathic, reiterative, and purposeful process.
- Rather than starting from what units you have to sell, what discounts your company may be offering, or prioritizing the most urgent leads, PCS plans advances for any qualified prospect regardless of their state of urgency or readiness.
- PCS planning begins and ends with a personal readiness perspective rather than mechanically relying on an assumed transactional progression that is supposed to convert a fixed

number of prospects (10 percent) by taking them from new leads to call-outs and then tour and close. If they do not close, the speed-to-lead process encourages that you move on to the next new lead. Quickly!

- PCS planning is most impactful if it is adopted as an important part of the ongoing sales team's culture with regularly scheduled daily sales meetings.

- Planning, and the time that it takes to plan, are critical and necessary sales conversion activities. As such, the time invested in planning next steps is included as a TSZ calculation.

- PCS planning should support and encourage sales counselors to empathetically connect with prospects and then try to untangle resistance using insightful questioning. This is far more effective than "surface fishing," which uses discovery only to identify the most urgent leads. Done well, planning next steps for individual prospects motivates sales counselors, boosts team building, and creates an energized, supportive, collaborative forum that will help your team build their sales skills.[62] Done well, it will also be fun.

Keep in mind that next steps with PCS are not thought of as a tactic. It's about planning meaningful questions and areas of inquiry that will help the prospect explore based on advancing readiness. Only after targeting a readiness strategy do effective PCS planners consider the best method to engage: by phone, email, tour, social media, etc.[63]

---

[62] Unlike trying to meet quotas for sales tasks and activities, exploring the prospect's life story also appears to help "generate achievement drive, motivation, and excitement with the sales team." See Willingham, R. (2003). *Integrity Selling for the 21st Century: How to Sell the Way People Want to Buy.* New York: Doubleday. pp. 106-119.

[63] Table 4 from David Smith & Alexandra Fisher (2012). "Measuring Success in Seniors Housing Sales: Prospect-Centered Selling® with the 'Stages of Change' Model", *Seniors Housing & Care Journal, p. 33.*

Unlike most sales scenario planning, PCS planning begins by minimizing or ignoring stated objections and the transactional history of the prospect with our community. Transactional sellers usually start their prospect review planning by recounting the sales history, namely, "Here's all the things I did," or stated objections, "I tried really hard, but they still said no because…" Instead, PCS planning does not take the facts or objections as given by the prospect literally. We understand that the prospect is often responding more with emotions than with logic or reason. We reinforce this understanding in the prospect case study by first considering the prospect's biography and life story as well as any information about readiness or motivations before reviewing what we did or how they objected. The idea is to create a picture or profile of who the prospect is, how they see themselves, and what they value before we examine their sales history or objections.

DAILY SESSIONS TO PLAN READINESS ADVANCES FOR INDIVIDUAL PROSPECTS

I've always found it very impactful to engage in daily group planning or brainstorming sessions. Every day. First thing in the morning for at least an hour or so. Planning and brainstorming before and after each prospect interaction makes an enormous impact on your sales counselors' probabilities for success.

It is helpful to have a dedicated space for planning, set up as a *situation room* or *war room*. The situation room works best if physically separated from a discovery room. The situation room is to the discovery room what a kitchen is to a dining room. Here is where, each day, the sales team works, convenes for daily sales meetings, does collaborative planning, and keeps track of their leads. From here the team launches CFU campaigns for each of the key prospects on their *top-10 board*.

Most importantly, it's a place to brainstorm, collaborate, have fun, and be creative. Every element in the situation room is designed to create a sense of urgency and should be stocked with items like grease boards and visual tools that are conducive to sharing ideas, promoting focus, planning, and developing proactive selling initiatives.

A brainstorming, case-study-based approach to the planning process requires both preparation and practice. When trying to build trust with prospects to connect and when asking them tough, awkward questions about their feelings, most sales counselors have their own fears, like fear of intimacy, failure, or rejection. Counselors with a high EQ have the courage to be vulnerable enough to question ask clarifying questions about a prospect's fears. Ongoing group PCS practice allows the selling team to explore multiple possible scenarios in a safe environment. Group pre-planning helps define engagement targets and build counselor confidence for actual prospect engagements. It warms up and continues to build upon the team's "selling muscles."

During daily group planning sessions, we also look for what is not being said by the prospect. Like a good attorney, we try to identify or at least hypothesize about the core emotional issues that may be blocking a logical decision. Hypothetical PCS planning is the best way we know of to prepare and practice what could happen during a face-to-face, voice-to-voice, or delivery of a personalized CFU. Preparation helps calm the counselor's mind and build confidence. It also allows our sales teams to consider multiple possible scenarios, develop a customized readiness strategy, think of meaningful questions appropriate for their situation, and determine what kind of advance might be possible.

PCS focuses and invests time planning for individual prospects, one at a time.

PCS focuses and invests time planning for individual prospects, one at a time. Five elements characterize the overall prioritization and workflows of effective PCS planning: choose which prospects to focus on, challenge assumptions and explore possibilities, consider strategic next steps, consider and rank viable tactics, and rank your advance possibilities by factors such as importance, probable impact, and degree of difficulty.

Prioritize Which Prospects to Focus On

In practice, nearly all established senior living communities have too many leads and too little time to properly plan. Yes, too many fully qualified, higher-functioning prospects just aren't ready yet. It's important, then, to consider who should we invest our limited amount of TSZ to work with.

Early on in my work as a sales counselor, I learned to stay on top of planning next steps for about 10 prospects at a time. It didn't have to be 10 exactly, but 10, plus or minus a few, was the goal. That's not to say you shouldn't continue to promptly respond to new inquires or nurture all of your prospects. It's more of a guideline for how you spend the majority of your time planning.

Which 10 should you choose? This question has always been challenging for me. As a hands-on sales counselor, I'm confident that if you present me with 10 qualified IL rental prospects, I'll close five of them. I will probably get an even better percentage in a higher-acuity setting. It's way more challenging for me, however, to predict which 50 percent I'll close and which will choose to stay home.

At Sherpa, we're currently building an algorithm that uses around 30 discrete factors plus ongoing machine learning to help us predict which prospects are most likely to buy. It will automatically score the lead base prospects with criteria that include recent advances, assessed stage of readiness, number of face-to-face and voice-to-voice interactions (and for how long), number of planning sessions, CFU, initial source of lead, etc. The algorithm will provide some guidance as to who we may be more likely to advance, and with automated machine learning, the predictions will continue to get sharper and more granular over time.

In general, a practical guideline for choosing which prospects to focus on first relies on an adaptation of Steven Covey's grid of urgency and importance.[64] Per Covey, the most effective performers start with tending to that which is both "urgent" and "important." That would include any face-to-face engagements for the near future or a new inquiry. Next up for top performers, according to Covey, are things that are "not urgent" but are "very important" to achieving your goals. In a senior living sales scenario, this would include planning for next steps and personalized CFU. These are not urgent because the initiative for these behaviors must be internal. No one is expecting or waiting for us to plan or follow up.

What Covey urges us to avoid, as much as possible, is focusing on what's not important to meeting our goals, especially the not important things that are urgent. Urgent but not important scenarios might include a walk-in from a family member of someone who is already sold, a resident who needs something attended to, or participation in a marketing event where you already have more than 15 leads per vacant unit.

Create and Review a Meaningful Sales Journal

Effective planning begins by creating a meaningful prospect profile, assessing their current stage of readiness, and then developing a personalized strategy designed to advance their readiness. We were strongly committed to doing proactive planning for next steps and frustrated with the existing templates and recording tools. For solutions, I first looked

---

[64] Covey, Stephen, *The 7 Habits of Highly Effective People* (1998), Free Press.

back to my legal experience and then to medical SOAP journaling for a more effective way to create a prospect profile.

1. Content Organization Models:
The Legal Brief and SOAP Journaling

In law school, we used case studies or legal briefs to create meaningful and accepted formats for recording and organizing facts. They are a necessary aid that helps encapsulate and analyze the mountains of material that lawyers must digest. The legal brief represents a final product after reviewing a set of facts or reading a published case, rereading it, taking it apart, and putting it back together again. In addition to its function as a tool for self-instruction and reference, the legal brief also provided a valuable summary of what you could call a cheat sheet.

This format for gathering, storing, and interpreting content learned is a consistent way to communicate and discuss discovery, outcomes, and opinions and to analyze implications. Physicians use a comparable problem-solving approach to journaling medical records called the SOAP note. Facts are organized into four sections: subjective, objective, assessment, and plan. Medical documentation is a vital part of the treatment process. SOAP notes were designed to facilitate better treatment plans and allowed clinicians to communicate with a common language and purpose.

2. Prospect-Centered Sales Case Study Template

In order to construct strategic action plans to help senior living prospects move through the continuum of change, we needed a means of organizing sales journal entries. Like doctors, lawyers, and other trained professionals, it is critical to maintain a prospect sales journal organized in concise, meaningful *content buckets* to help guide planning for next steps and follow-up. Rather than bury bits of discovery into sequentially organized records that chronicle *what we did*, PCS organizes *information that we have discovered* at various times during our multiple prospect engagements into four primary content buckets, each associated with one of the four stages of readiness for change.[65] Not so coincidentally, guidelines for questioning techniques at any particular stage are the same as Neil Rackham's recommended SPIN questioning sequence.

Here are the four content buckets:

- **Biography or Situation**, which includes a prospect's life story, legacy, themes, and values, as well as their typical day and qualifiers. These were designed to help us connect and to draw out prospects in denial and make use of Rackham's "situational" questions.
- **Motivators,** which present problems in a prospect's current living situation. These statements relate to helping the prospect in the thinking stage articulate why they should move rather than stay. They also make use of Rackham's "problem" questions.
- **Objections** are stated concerns or implications about moving now. By referring to these objections, a counselor can help prospects in the planning stage to assess the advantages of moving sooner rather than later. Questions here differ a little from Rackham's "implication" questions. Instead, following Prochaska and the psychologists, we use these questions to help draw out the prospect's story and examine the implications of moving forward. They focus on perceived risks, which are usually in the form of objections.

---

[65] In 2014 when we launched Sherpa, our unique, bifurcated journaling went digital. The key prospect profile templates replicated and enhanced the manual journaling systems that we created during multiple One On One turnaround campaigns. This patented Sherpa workflow allows the user to track activity, use of time, and outcomes in a separate section of the journal from what they discover and what information they need to plan next steps.

- **Preferences** are designed for prospects in the action stage and compare the features and benefits of alternate options. We use Rackham's "need payoff" questions here.

Organizing discovery into content buckets also helps us discover what we don't know or what questions might inspire and guide the prospect to advance.

3. Get the Full Picture of Prospects and Influencers

In Sherpa, the presence of information in each content bucket is summarized with avatars. This provides a visual summary of meaningful readiness content areas that we know about, as well as the ones that merit further discovery. The template becomes a summary of our discovery and a road map for additional questions and exploration. Completing the case study content buckets is like creating a reverse dating site profile. We enter what the prospect says in response to our discovery, creating a profile that reflects their own words. Emotional ambivalence and self-persuasion occur based not on what sales counselors say but rather on the prospect telling us about their motivations, sources of resistance, and personal preferences.

We find it impactful to include photos of the prospect and other members of the buying team in prospect profiles. The visual reference helps the salesperson connect more meaningfully and turn the "lead" into a real person. We were able to substantiate the effectiveness of this practice with data from the ProMatura-Sherpa study; including a photo significantly improved a salesperson's level of engagement and success.

This idea has been tested and proven in studies from other disciplines. For example, in a controlled study, a medical researcher gave some hospital radiologists a set of complex X-rays to look at and assess.[66] Then, they gave another group the same set of images, only this time they

---

[66] https://www.press.rsna.org/timssnet/media/pressreleases/pr_target.cfm?ID=389

included a picture of the patient. Accuracy results went up by 80 percent. Viewing the patient—or in our case, the prospect—as a "real person" has a positive impact on results.

I've found that nearly every prospect wants to be photographed. They want to be "seen." The biggest obstacles that I encountered in taking a prospect photo were resistance not from the prospects but from the sales counselors, who were afraid of being too pushy. In my experience, that is nearly always a projection from the sales counselor onto the prospect they want to photograph. Getting permission to take a prospect's photo is actually pretty simple. You just have to first earn their trust and show them that their story and their life has made an impact on you.

Pictures of prospects provide visual memory. If I've worked with a prospect like Mitch, I'll remember a lot of the stories he's told by seeing his picture, without having to recall and recite a lot of situational or biological data. For the lowest performers in our study, only about 7 percent of their leads had prospect pictures. For the highest performers, more than 18 percent had prospect photos.

For the lowest performers in our study, only about 7 percent of their leads had prospect pictures. For the highest performers, more than 18 percent had prospect photos.

4. Challenge Logical Assumptions and Explore Possibilities

During daily interactive prospect case study sessions with your team, you'll focus on about 10 prospects. Preferably, your community's ED, sales leader, counselors, and one or more community-level department heads will be there. At that meeting, our sales team would discuss what stage of readiness we thought "cold" prospects like Fred and Rose had reached. Relying on our impressions from the sales journal as well as our counselor's recollection, we assessed Fred as being either in complete denial or in the thinking stage.

Logically, it made little sense to stay after their doctor told them that Rose's declining health necessitated them moving into an AL community. However, Fred wasn't seeing the logic. Our choice was to assume we could eventually convince and persuade Fred that Rose's health risk was reason enough to move, whether he was ready or not. But Fred wasn't going to make decisions or agree to change anything based on logic. He didn't even trust the facts. "Maybe the doctor had it all wrong and I don't have Alzheimer's. Certainly, we can make it for a few more years. Besides, what would we do with all of our stuff?" Fred seemed to have an answer, however illogical, to each of our proposed solutions. Instead, he was following the themes built into a deeply emotional story.

During a planning session, we collaborate with each other. We don't discuss which apartment floor plan to offer or whether to give a discount. Rather, our intention during a planning session is to discover ways to connect with the prospect's story on an emotional level. The only way to help Fred untangle his fear of moving and losing his adventurous identity was to probe into his life story, trying to understand what he was feeling and which emotions might require untangling.

During a planning session, we collaborate with each other.

After assessing what stage Fred was in, we explored possibilities for helping him advance. What kinds of questions would help him start confronting his ambivalence? Instead of trying to argue away his conclusions with situational logic, we went with the emotional skid. Maybe the doctors were wrong. Did Fred believe that? Was Fred concerned about Rose's ability to be his caregiver? Should he be? Did he even need caregiving? If so, for what? Couldn't they just engage a part-time caregiver? How would Fred react if we gave him a model of one of the airplanes he used to fly? In other words, we gave up our logical assumptions and followed the story driving Fred's emotional decision-making.

Planning sessions may or may not lead you to solutions. By collaborating toward advancing readiness, regardless of the sales result, we become more invested in and more motivated to try to help prospects get ready. Open, purposeful planning sessions also provide focused conversational warm-ups, identify underlying questions, and provide us with a live daily forum not only to plan advances but also to practice clarifying and awareness-provoking questioning options. PCS planning is selling. It is impactful both before and after physical or digital engagements. Planning helps give senior living sales counselors their own chance to "get ready."

5. Evaluate Possible Next Steps

To move your prospects toward readiness, take small steps, and don't be afraid to be creative in your approach. In Fred and Rose's case, we assessed Fred as being in thinking and Rose in planning. Our strategic plan began with helping Fred, who was furthest away from being ready, to explore why he would consider moving. We did this in the context of his personal history.

Actionable next steps might be:

Action Plan Options
Strategic Goal: Help Fred move from thinking to planning stage
Build discrepancy around staying home with Fred during a home visit
Offer to help with downsizing with a moving plan or garage sale
Bring Fred a model airplane
Offer to purchase their home
Send a heartfelt letter and give them copies for their adult children

Discuss each possibility as a group and determine whether you think targeting that goal will advance Fred and Rose's readiness to buy. Since this activity is somewhat subjective, collaborative discussion, brainstorming, and consensus among the team will help. Clarify options and raise relevant questions that need to be addressed as part of the plan.

Once you have identified a target objective that, if achieved, will advance the sale, consider whether it will be easy or hard for the prospect to agree to it. Rank these choices based on difficulty level. For example, it's easier to send Fred and Rose flowers and a note than it is to request a home visit. How realistic are your proposed actions? What can you do now, and what will need time to achieve?

Although not generally promoted or tracked by transactional sellers, purposeful planning of next steps for individual prospects most certainly constitutes selling. It has a huge impact on conversions.

Prioritize your options, and record your next steps. For Fred and Rose, we started by delivering a model airplane and requesting a home visit. Here's how we recorded these stages in our Action Plan worksheet, which we adapted from Rackham's *SPIN Selling*:

	Lead to an Advance?	Easy or hard?	Rank choices
Invite for event	No		
Request home visit	Yes	5	After flowers
Ask for the deposit	No		
Contact daughter	Maybe	3	Fallback
Send flowers and note	Yes	1	First

6. Build Momentum from Recent Advances

Remember, advances reflect how we bridge the gap between "I'm not ready" and "I wish I would have moved sooner." Take small steps, one after another. Research shows that each prospect advance increases the probability of another one later on. Each advance increases the prospect's readiness to buy.

It's important to track key metrics related to advances:

- The number and type of advances
- Your time spent planning advances
- Whether you have meaningful, readiness-oriented next steps for each person you engage

Setting goals for reaching at least two or three advances per day helps you to prioritize your planning sessions and strategies. Goals for readiness-oriented advances also provide you and your prospect with a sense of achievement along the way. Find a simple way to celebrate your advances.

Goals for readiness-oriented advances also provide you and your prospect with a sense of achievement along the way. Find a simple way to celebrate your advances.

We ring a bell or tap a gong in the sales office, but you could also have an impromptu dance party, send a celebratory email, or just go nuts!

A focus on planning meaningful readiness advances in senior living moves your sales team from wandering generalities to actionable next steps by planning for and then executing meaningful specifics. It helps us focus on specific, prospect-oriented goals that target and facilitate a change before offering product-related solutions. The probability of you getting additional or multiple advances increases when you not only have a personalized, well-planned readiness strategy but also when you employ high-impact tactics such as home visits, personalized CFU, and leadership from the ED.

Presence of at Least One Planning Activity

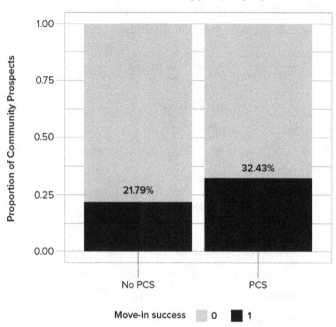

Proportion of Prospects to Move-In by
Presence of Planning (Sherpa-Wylde)

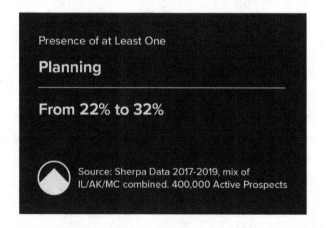

Presence of at Least One

Planning

From 22% to 32%

Source: Sherpa Data 2017-2019, mix of
IL/AK/MC combined. 400,000 Active Prospects

CHAPTER 9

High-Impact Tactics

Nothing in the world can take the place of perseverance.
Talent will not; nothing is more common than unsuccessful men
with talent. Genius will not; unrewarded genius is almost a proverb.
Education will not; the world is full of educated derelicts.
Persistence and determination are omnipotent.

—Calvin Coolidge

Our sales strategy is always to use connection and untangling to build readiness to buy. This readiness challenges emotional resistance in favor of making a reasoned buying decision. Advances occur when we motivate prospects to advance through distinct stages of change. Daily planning sessions help clarify next steps in the prospect's readiness journey. Sales tactics are the ways that we execute our readiness strategy. They are ways of engaging and interacting with prospects at any stage. Some are more impactful in terms of driving advances than others.

Research from 2016 by ProMatura Group[67] identified the relative benefit of six different tactics used by highly effective sales professionals. Each was scored based on its relative impact on prospects who moved

---

[67] The results of this study were published in a Sherpa Senior Housing News white paper, *Sales Enablement in Senior Living: A Roadmap to an Effective and Sustainable Sales Culture,* a copy of which can be obtained at: https://resources.seniorhousingnews.com/a-roadmap-to-an-effective-and-sustainable-sales-culture. Sponsored by ASHA. The study examined data from more than 300,000 sales encounters of 500-plus sales counselors.

in. These activities showed an increase in conversions in the following percentages: face-to-face (39 percent), voice-to-voice (call-in 15 percent and call-out 2 percent), planning (19 percent), CFU (23 percent), and email/mail (5 percent).

Whichever tactics you employ with a higher-functioning prospect, it's hardly ever one and done. IL prospects generally take five to seven advances before committing to move. Most all of those attempts to engage usually end in failure or rejection. Perseverance and persistence are among the ingredients needed to prove we really care about our prospects. Some refer to this selfless effort as "empathic concern." It is the foundational element for heroic selling.

The focus of this chapter is on how to use high-impact tactics to get a better picture of who our prospects are and fill in the sometimes lengthy gaps between onsite tours and voice-to-voice engagements.

HOME VISITS

Intent of Home Visits

Presence of at Least One Home Visit

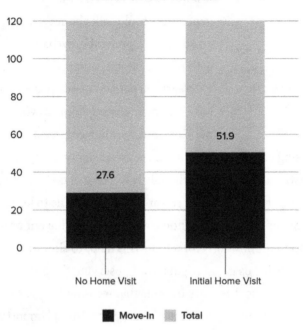

Proportion of Prospects to Move-In by
Presence of Home Visit Status

Move-In   Total

Presence of at Least One

Home Visit

From 28% to 52%

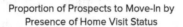

Source: Sherpa Data 2017-2019, mix of
IL/AK/MC combined. 400,000 Active Prospects

The silent generation, our current prospects' generation, is used to slower, more personal interactions. Their doctors, lawyers, bankers, and insurance agents (anyone important) did house calls, meaning they would visit their clients at home. It was expected that people from this generation could talk about serious things on an adult level, preferably eyeball to eyeball and with more characters than Twitter permits.

> The silent generation, our current prospects' generation, is used to slower, more personal interactions.

Nearly 90 percent of prospects in your lead base see their existing home as your real competition, not another community. Naturally, most leasing counselors visit all of the other senior living competitors in our market. So why not personally take a tour of their existing home? Through experience and data research, we have come to learn that it is even more impactful to make home visits before asking our prospects to come into the community for a tour. This helps to slow down the interaction and helps us gain insights from observing the prospect in their own environment. These are insights that we wouldn't get elsewhere.

People feel comfortable in their home. They also feel important when someone takes time out of their day to come to them. A home visit gives prospects a chance to describe their life, values, and fears while in their own environment. Six weeks after a prospect we'll call Bob moved into a senior living community in Sharonville, Ohio, he said, "They hardly ever talked to me on the phone. No, they preferred to talk to me in my home, which was miles away from their place. For somebody to come all the way out here just to talk, to me, says a lot. That's probably what closed me on this job."

When you go on a home visit, be sure to bring along a presentation book, your computer, or a tablet with sales collateral like pictures or renderings, floor plans, price lists, testimonials, or any other materials. Also bring a box of candy, flowers, or some other gift. Your goal should be to further the relationship and get a decision or advance of some kind. Try to schedule another small commitment before you leave, and always bring a complete lease package, just in case!

Your goal should be to further the relationship and to get a decision or advance of some kind.

Being on their own turf, prospects are generally more open to exploring their thoughts and feelings about moving than they would on a tour of our community. Take your time. The more you learn about your prospects and their emotional needs, the more they will build trust for your input. It is also motivating for counselors to better understand a prospect's current situation, their resistance to change, and perhaps what benefits they will gain by moving to your community. Even more important is that drawing out the prospect's feelings about moving and letting go of their current lifestyle helps the prospect untangle current reality from deep-seated legacy stories.

A prospect's home is often the very best setting to discover important information. Look around. How big is the yard? Are they keeping up with housekeeping and home maintenance? Are there stairs? How far are the nearest shopping area, church, and hospital? Is the neighborhood safe? How would you feel about your parent living there?

Being in the prospect's home gives you a great opportunity to observe a lot about what they are interested in, how much furniture they may need to get rid of, and how well they function on their own. You may also learn a great deal about their family members, community involvement, and financial circumstances.

You might feel uncomfortable broaching personal topics, especially if the prospect is simply calling around to get information from multiple communities. You may feel like you're invading their privacy. They may not be used to being offered a home visit as part of the sale. But there are a few things that can establish a genuine connection between two people before and after the home visit.

You establish trust early on by letting the prospect know that you are not there to "sell" to them and that home visits are part of the process of learning about them and helping them make this important, life-changing decision.

You establish trust early on by letting the prospect know that you are not there to "sell" to them and that home visits are part of the process of learning about them and helping them make this important, life-changing decision.[68] Make sure you do this early in the initial inquiry stages by clearly stating your intentions. It can sound as simple and professional as this:

Here in our community, it's our practice to offer to visit you and chat in the comfort of your own home. My intention is to be a guide to you and your family, regardless of whether you choose to move or not. Would you be open to me coming over and bringing some lunch?

The main reason it can feel awkward to ask for a home visit is that many of us are afraid that prospects will think of us as salespeople. And no counselor wants a salesperson to pitch them anywhere, but especially not at home. However, on the contrary, we have found most senior prospects are delighted to have someone care enough to go to their home. A well-planned home visit can be the key differentiator between you and other senior living communities. But be advised, you may encounter some unusual situations during home visits. Every home visit is an adventure of sorts. Expect the unexpected.

LEARNING FROM A HOME VISIT: ARLENE

During a turnaround, rapid-fill campaign in Chicago, we couldn't advance a sale with Arlene, a prospect who was in her late 70s. We all found her to be an elegant and intelligent woman. She acknowledged

---

[68] If you are primarily working with an adult child, you may also offer to visit to them somewhere besides your community. Set the expectation that you are happy to meet them somewhere convenient like near their workplace. You can also hand-deliver information or documents at a coffee shop and offer to walk through the details with them personally.

that she was having a number of problems living alone. Yet in earlier conversations and on an initial tour, Arlene convinced us that she was still "very independent."

Like many other prospects, Arlene's daughter had been urging her mom to make a change. Arlene said she loved our community. If she ever moved anywhere, it would be to our place. "But I wouldn't possibly even consider moving as long as I can still drive," she said.

It was with this perspective that instead of relegating her to the cold lead bin, we tried for a home visit. It was an opportunity to establish trust and see what was really happening.

When we arrived, we could see that Arlene's house and adjoining garage sat on a steep-grade driveway with a mailbox at the bottom. As a courtesy, we collected her mail and walked up the hill to knock on the door. She was most appreciative. When we later discussed her fear of falling, we asked how she navigated her trip to the mailbox every day, and Arlene took us out to the garage, where a dark blue vintage Buick was parked.

"Usually, I just back down to the mailbox with my car," she told us. "That's mostly what my driving these days is limited to. I use a taxi for all my errands." We noticed a long dent along the passenger side of the Buick, from bumper to bumper. It was the same height as the brick retaining wall that ran the length of the driveway. We finally understood what she meant by "I'm still driving."

We offered to put the dinner we'd brought in Arlene's fridge. One look and we learned more about what she meant by "still living independently." The only food inside was several boxes of leftovers from a local restaurant and a large, ornate serving bowl filled with leftover Halloween candy bars. These discoveries helped us identify discrepancies between Arlene's ideas of independence and the realities of her current situation. Establishing trust helped us talk about them without judgment.

PERSONALIZED CREATIVE FOLLOW-UP

C FU is probably the most underutilized yet most impactful sales conversion tool we have. Except for face-to-face interactions, this is the most critical and effective, and least expensive, way to bond with prospects. It builds familiarity, trust, and intimacy.

CFUs can be physical objects or something extraordinary that you do, like joining them on a visit to a competitor community, cooking one of their favorite recipes, writing a crossword puzzle or poem, sending a heartfelt letter with radical candor, or solving problems for them that exceed your expected role as a salesperson.

CFU refers to a myriad of relentless, personalized, provocative selling initiatives to connect with prospects, gain their trust, and motivate their willingness to engage. Each personalized follow-up initiative should be an intimate, one-of-a-kind gesture that communicates, "I see you and accept you just as you are, and I want to take the time to celebrate that."

Why do they work? Because instead of standardized sales tactics, these are *individualized* and *surprising.*[69] Note that CFUs are a tactic, a means to follow up with prospects who "aren't ready yet." CFUs are an important tactic to motivate readiness for change in higher-functioning prospects. An effective follow-up campaign will nurture your existing qualified leads. It will be:

- **Cost Effective:** CFUs are always more cost-effective than marketing or public relations strategies that focus on generating more new inquiries. Moreover, use of CFUs to improve

---

[69] In my 1995 *Guerilla Sales Tool Kit,* I wrote that personalized follow-up "means you don't have any rules to follow. There's no 'one size fits all' or 'one style for everybody' in terms of prospects. They come in all shapes and sizes and personalities with all different kinds of needs and in order to get through you've got to be amazing and outrageous. You have to be accessible and surprising because each relationship will build and develop and grow differently. The common thread in each and every case is letting the prospect know just how much you care and personalizing your efforts."

conversion ratios will reduce overall costs for new lead generation.

- **Proactive:** You maintain complete control over timing, format, and costs.
- **Persuasive:** Sending something, even if it has already been discussed face to face or over the phone, helps further the selling process. Your prospect can react and interact in their own time frame and in their own setting. Personalized follow-up has a persuasive selling power or "ghost" effect that works even when you are not physically present.

Low-Cost, High-Impact Persuasion: Bea and the Paper Napkin

It was the invisible ghost effect, a kind of silent, persuasive challenger, that finally persuaded Bea to move from New Mexico back to her roots in Oklahoma City. We were doing a turnaround of a 25-year-old IL/AL community. Bea was a delightful 76-year-old retired social worker who came in for a last-minute tour with her two daughters. She was scheduled to return to New Mexico the next night.

We spent several hours touring, talking, and discussing whether it made sense to move back to her hometown. Both daughters were impressed with our community and very enthusiastic about their mom moving in. Bea seemed curious but apprehensive. "I just don't know what to do. I need more time to think about my options," she said.

Before she left, I took a paper napkin that was on the table and drew a line down the middle. On one side, and in her own words, we wrote down 10 of the benefits that she would have if she were to move back to Oklahoma City. She said that her current situation was difficult to keep up, and it was wearing her down. A move to a senior community like ours would make life a lot easier.

In the second column, we added corresponding rows numbered 1 to 10 for Bea to write down the advantages of her staying in New Mexico without moving. She couldn't think of any on the spot. I suggested a couple. She wouldn't have to move or get new doctors if she stayed. While still curious to explore benefits with me further, Bea needed to leave and get ready for her trip home. As we said our goodbyes, I encouraged her to take the napkin with her. "Write down the advantages of staying when you think of some," I suggested. She agreed, thanked me, and put the napkin in her purse.

By 10:00 the next morning, she called me from Albuquerque. "David, I've been staring at that damn napkin all night trying to come up with valid reasons not to move," she told me. "It surprises me, but I couldn't come up with a single one. I'm still a little scared, but what the heck? Would you please send me a lease for that two-bedroom apartment we saw yesterday?"

If something interesting or important comes up during a phone call or visit, take note or ask for details. The more that your CFU reflects the prospect's unique values, the more the materials will be evocative and impactful. Making connections based on personally significant factors is important at any stage of the sale process, but especially when they promote additional face-to-face or voice-to-voice connections and inspire breakthroughs and changes in attitude.

CFUs are appropriate at any time. It should be on your mind as soon you've finished your first phone conversation or any meaningful interaction. Continue building up CFU ideas throughout the entire selling process.[70] To help create more prospect urgency, follow up urgently yourself. Deliver CFUs while you're on the way to work. Call a courier.

---

[70] To help generate prospect responses at every stage of change and even from otherwise "cold" prospects like Ed and Rose, employ what Jay Conrad Levinson, Guerilla Marketing (1983), calls "Personalized, surprising, and proactive selling initiatives."

Presence of at Least One Creative Follow-Up

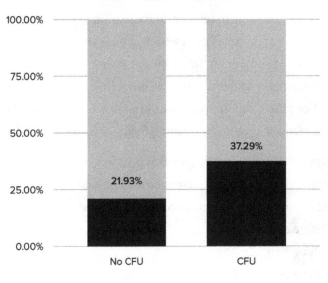

Proportion of Prospects to Move-In by
Presence of Creative Follow-Up

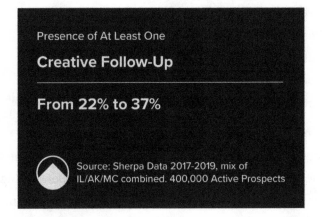

Presence of At Least One

Creative Follow-Up

From 22% to 37%

Source: Sherpa Data 2017-2019, mix of
IL/AK/MC combined. 400,000 Active Prospects

Use overnight delivery. Send the community limo to bring brochures to your prospects. Whatever you do for follow-up, do it today instead of tomorrow. Acting urgently sends a message to the prospect: "I care about your quality of life. This is serious business!"

Your goal should be to send or do something to each of your top 10 leads at least several times per week. To be effective, CFUs need to be continuous. Do something before and/or after every face-to-face visit. Respond whenever something special, interesting, or unusual comes up in a visit or phone call. Initiate some kind of CFU whenever the sales scenario seems to have lost direction, focus, or energy:

- After an inquiry from a qualified prospect or adult child
- After you get a yes to an appointment request
- After you get a no to an appointment request
- Before a tour
- After a tour
- After a phone call
- As a retouch when you haven't reached out for a while

When planning CFUs, how intimate should you be? Identify these factors first:

- Level of knowledge and trust
- Prospect's stage of readiness to make a move
- Prospect's personality or sense of humor
- Whether you are reaching out to an adult child
- Whether you are reaching out for professional referrals

If there is a low level of knowledge and trust, err on the side of doing something that comes across as fun but is also tied to something special about the person. It should be inspirational. Avoid sending things with your company/community logo. Don't give information relating to the product unless they have requested it.

Flowers, books, personal notes, or something inspired by a conversation you had with them are always great places to start. Play to the prospect's personality, style, and life story. The impact of any CFU is improved if you use the CFU to acknowledge who they are. Start with the message you want to send them. Then craft the CFU to speak directly to them personally.

If there is a high level of knowledge and trust, you should have enough discovery to create something meaningful and personalized for them in a CFU.

For example, when sending a CFU to a prospect who is a lawyer, I may use legal language to create a petition filed by our community. The petition would be formatted like a formal court document. The body of the complaint would state relevant background information about the prospect's situation, as well as problems and motivators taken from the prospect's legacy story. Like all legal petitions, it would end with a request (called a prayer) for the court to order something. Our CFU petitions pray for a chance to visit the prospect in their home, for a tour, or for whatever other advance is appropriate. It would be as professional-looking as possible but with the intention to get a laugh.

Example of Low-Trust, Low-Knowledge CFU:
Mary S. and Wiggles

Here's a summary of my personal sales notes taken during an initial call-in and describing the CFU to Mary S. While we had very low levels of trust and knowledge, we took what we did know and labored to send something personal urgently.

Our first contact with Mary S. was on Saturday, November 12. She called at 6:00 p.m. She told us that she was currently residing in a retirement community in Naples, Florida, where she had lived for the past three years. She stated that she wanted to move back to St. Louis to be closer to her son.

Since she was already familiar with the lifestyle in a retirement community and our location in St. Louis, the issue for her was *where* rather than *whether* to move. During the initial call, she reported that her son was in Florida visiting and that they had been discussing various retirement community options in St. Louis. He was scheduled to leave the following afternoon.

We suspected that they had contacted several other communities that probably sent her brochures. We wanted to act urgently and have a high personal impact. During the conversation, Mary said she had a poodle named Wiggles who was a very important part of her life. Based on a quick review of our overall profile for Mary, we all agreed that she would be a great fit for our community.

After a group case study, we devised a CFU plan. We decided to show Mary that Wiggles was important to us—and that we were willing to prove it. We bought a basket of doggie treats and goodies at PetSmart. Back at the office, we made a pet basket and added a personal note. By the time we finished the basket, it was too late for a FedEx pickup. So we found air cargo transport leaving at 10:45 p.m. They would carry the package and deliver it to the Naples airport by early morning. We scheduled a taxi service in Naples and gave them pick-up and drop-off instructions.

The package arrived at Mary's place at 9:00 the next morning. She immediately called to thank us. Her son was equally impressed and visited upon his return to St. Louis. He selected an apartment on Mary's behalf. She sent us a deposit the following day.

Mary said that after receiving our package, she did not even consider looking anywhere else. The total cost of the CFU for Mary S. was way less than a quarter-page ad in the local papers:

PetSmart: $ 57.26
Air Cargo: $ 94.00
Taxi Service: $ 56.00

Total: $207.26

Example of a High-Level Trust, High-Knowledge CFU

Following is a CFU petition we sent to a retired judge and his wife after they toured. We did a home visit and had several phone conversations. We summarized the situation as we saw it. Notice the amount of detail that is being reflected back to the prospects. It's a form of radical candor formatted in a language that Judge Joe himself used for nearly 40 years.

State of Missouri
County of St. Louis
LIFESTYLE CIRCUIT
SENIOR DIVISION

The Gatesworth	)	In Re: Joseph S
	)	Alberta S
At One McKnight Place	)	
	)	
vs.	)	
	)	
Status Quo, a/k/a	)	Pending Lease #2020-470
Isolation	)	

PETITION

Comes now Petitioner, The Gatesworth at One McKnight Place ("The Gatesworth") with respect to the matter of Judge Joseph S and his wife Alberta and for its action against the status quo, also known as "Isolation," states as follows:

1. Joe is a very smart, articulate, and delightful retired law professor and judge. He and his delightful wife, retired teacher Alberta, currently live at xxx East Lockwood Ave, in St Louis, Missouri. They are financially well off and health-qualified for independent living.

2. Since losing his office at the University Law School, Joe has some ongoing health needs and has lost the desire to keep up with engaging with colleagues, exploring and experiencing life as much as he has in the past. Alberta has become a caregiver. She would like to paint again but doesn't have a studio. She is also in need of some socialization.

3. Joe's longtime friend, Kenny R, is concerned about Joe and Alberta's well-being. He has investigated various living options including The Gatesworth. He believes that Joe and Alberta's quality of life will be significantly enhanced by moving to The Gatesworth. On Joe's behalf, Kenny negotiated some discounts and concessions with one of the owners.

4. Nevertheless, Joe and Alberta have not yet made up their minds to move and are still considering bringing in home health care aides or simply waiting until some crisis or emergency forces him to move into a skilled nursing home.

5. Joe and Alberta's daughter, Sue, is a practicing attorney. She has visited The Gatesworth with her parents, would very much like to see them move, and has reviewed and approved all of the paperwork.

Now therefore, Petitioner prays on behalf of Judge Joseph and Alberta S for an order declaring that they immediately accept the generous Trial Stay offer, sign the Residence Agreement and Addendum, make a one-month fully refundable deposit, and give life at The Gatesworth a reasonable chance.

Respectfully submitted,

David A. Smith
And the entire Team
The Gatesworth
One McKnight Place
St. Louis, Missouri 63132

This petition provoked a call-in, a good laugh, further conversation, a lease, and a move. That, in turn, led to a joyful Joe, Alberta, and daughter Sue.

Personalized CFU is the most critical and effective, and least expensive, way to connect and build trust with prospects. It builds familiarity and intimacy. Used consistently and creatively, CFUs will significantly increase conversion rates. Personalized follow-up isolates the real selling issues, fosters more of a sense of urgency, and often leads to additional face-to-face and voice-to-voice engagements.

Like home visits and planning, creation and execution of ongoing CFUs takes time and often assistance from other staff in the community. Cooperation and support from the ED are critical.

ORGANIZATIONAL TACTIC: MAKE THE ED THE SALES LEADER

To be sustainable, the commitment to improve sales effectiveness and wipe out vacancies using a prospect-readiness orientation, rather than an investor-centric perspective, must start at the top. The mission, culture, and success metrics of customer engagements need to be promoted and aligned at every level of the organization, from the investors to management and the on-site, community-level sales professionals.

In short, in terms of sales effectiveness, culture matters. Whatever the reasons, effective sales performance is currently undervalued in the senior living industry. One place that reflects this evaluation is in the fact that while the ED should be the CEO of the community, they rarely have any responsibilities to be accountable for occupancy. But they should. The ED's authority, credibility, and visibility enhance selling. Putting the ED into a sales leadership position also brings a strong, credible source of motivation and leadership to the sales staff and reassurance to prospects.

1. Consistent Messages and Reassurance to Prospects

There is a strange phenomenon in our industry: we treat our customers quite differently during the sales process than we do once they move in. It is like Dr. Jekyll and Mr. Hyde. Once they sign up, they became an actual person. Before they sign up, they are a "lead" or an "inquiry" that needs to get pushed through a sales funnel. The unintended message a higher-functioning prospect gets is, "We will really care about you once you move in and start paying us rent. Please understand that it is not part of our sales culture or methodology to *actually demonstrate* that we really care for you right now before you sign up."

There is a strange phenomenon in our industry: we treat our customers quite differently during the sales process than we do once they move in. It is like Dr. Jekyll and Mr. Hyde. Once they sign up, they became an actual person. Before they sign up, they are a "lead" or an "inquiry" that needs to get pushed through a sales funnel.

Let's consider a few common phrases in a typical senior housing mission statement and see whether they sync with our sales practices:

- **We are family:** Do we try to "sell" to our family?
- **We care:** How do we really demonstrate this when we are spending as little time as possible with each lead in an effort to move to the next one? Quotas lack compassion!
- **We honor your individuality:** But do speed-to-lead sellers truly honor prospect stories?
- **We value your independence:** Does our sales culture teach to convince and persuade, or do we serve as guides for prospects to make their own decision?
- **Our people make the difference:** Or are our salespeople just filling quotas and booking tours?

Fortunately, most senior living providers today boast a resident-centered approach with the ED driving the community's operating culture. There is a huge opportunity to also have the ED lead a prospect-centered approach in sales. However, all of our industry's currently accepted sales performance metrics scream the opposite.

2. Eliminate Marketing and Operations Silos

The most successful sales cultures eliminate artificial distinctions between marketing or sales and operations. Currently, many senior living portfolio operators tend to manage sales effectiveness by creating dual chains of authority that run from a national marketing director to regional and community-level managers. Generally, the marketing chain of command runs parallel to similarly organized operations or administrative staffing. Nearly all of the smaller independently owned and managed communities also keep marketing and management functions segregated from the hands-on or "trenches" level up to the very highest levels of management. In this model, the operations chain has all the authority and control, while the sales or marketing chains are primarily advisory. Nevertheless, the sales chains are generally where people are held accountable.

An essential key to executing more effective sales is to have the ED create a prospect-centered sales culture that is in sync with operations. A good first step is to eliminate artificial distinctions between marketing and operations. I found the most logical and cost-effective approach to sales leadership is to eliminate dual lines of authority by making the ED the "CEO" of the community. They are a CEO in that they are directly responsible for and therefore consistently involved with sales and marketing efforts on a daily basis.

ED TSZ Time Allocation

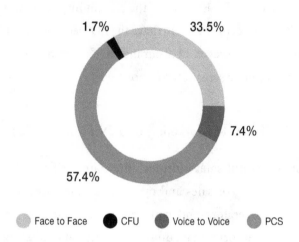

1.7%   33.5%

7.4%

57.4%

Face to Face   CFU   Voice to Voice   PCS

3. Supportive Work Culture

The senior leadership and investor stakeholders at many senior living companies today are still grounded in the antiquated speed-to-lead sales metrics for reporting and evaluating performance. Unfortunately, this perspective creates confusion with community-based sales teams that attempt to employ PCS. Cognitive dissonance often occurs when the sales counselor on-site, their ED, and/or their regional managers attempt to comply with two contradictory standards for sales effectiveness. People have an inherent desire to be consistent in their views, thoughts, and actions. When sales professionals are held to activity quotas based on getting more leads, tours, and call-outs, it creates stress and emotional discomfort. This may account for the whopping 50 percent-plus of senior living sales counselors who turn over each year.

The ED is also in a unique position to create and maintain a supportive customer-driven selling environment. All too often, the relationship that develops between the sales staff and those in operations is antagonistic or adversarial rather than supportive or cooperative: "Will you please cut a check for stamps and send a FedEx shipment? And would you serve lunch even if we are 15 minutes late?"

Left to fester, such conflict can impair everyone's selling effectiveness. The ED is in the best position to identify and eliminate selling barriers. They can offer creative responses to special client needs, relocate the space used for discovery and closing, help with targeting activities, and identify staff or other residents to assist in the selling scenario. They can also help by relocating, refurbishing, or eliminating model apartments.

4. Hands-On Knowledge Leads to Higher NOI

Unfortunately, most owner-operators do not task, enable, or encourage the ED to lead or have any more than a superficial involvement in the sales process. During our turnaround consulting days, Alex and I conducted a survey to determine the title or position of the people who had direct, hands-on responsibility for sales results in rental retirement communities. We were surprised to find that despite the numerous advantages of hands-on ED involvement, the elimination of vacancies was not even mentioned as a key responsibility by 60 percent of the EDs interviewed. Moreover, over 75 percent of EDs could not state the names, statuses, or action plans for any of their communities' best prospective residents.

As evidenced by our survey data, too often, senior management and owners lose touch with what's happening in the selling trenches. Hands-on involvement by the ED, however, affords an objective and realistic window into what's happening there. Management's involvement also ensures a better assessment of budgeting and personnel needs, pricing and special incentive strategies, and special prospect needs. Getting the ED directly in touch with incoming prospects is a cost-effective way to avoid what Jim Moore refers to as "positioning myopia" or a "lack of vision for realistic planning for the future."[71]

Finally, the ED can support sales counselors by:

- Providing resources like a library of CFU supplies and establishing a supportive CFU budget.
- Helping set reasonable goals for TSZ and how to invest it.
- Minimizing obstacles to help sales counselors spend as much TSZ as possible.
- Participating actively in prospect planning sessions.
- Whenever possible, meeting and visiting with prospects during tours or events.
- Recognizing small successes and advances, not just move-ins.

Senior living sales strategies identify opportunities to advance readiness along an evidence-based continuum. Advancing in small steps increases the probability of getting additional advances. The impact of each strategic initiative is amplified with the use of high-impact tactics. Specifically, home visits and personalized CFUs are what advance readiness during time gaps in between tours, phone calls, and email interactions. These high-impact tactics drive higher conversion rates. Enlisting the ED to directly participate in and provide ongoing oversight of the sales effort enriches and elevates a person-centered culture in sales and operations.

---

[71] Moore, James, *Assisted Living Strategies for Changing Markets*, Westbridge Publishing (2001).

CONCLUSION

E veryone's life is a story. Customers don't want to be told a story by you and your team. What is more effective is for the counselor to think of each prospect as the protagonist in their own life story. Downsizing into a senior living community is a unique and challenging experience. Our potential customers, prospects like Mitch, Fred, or Rose, are people who may or may not occupy vacant apartments, but they are for sure human beings who have a strong need to tell their stories, just like we all do. Heroic sellers thrive on helping them tell and make sense out of those stories.

> Our potential customers, prospects like Mitch, Fred, or Rose, are people who may or may not occupy vacant apartments, but they are for sure human beings who have a strong need to tell their stories, just like we all do. Heroic sellers thrive on helping them tell and make sense out of those stories.

With PCS, we want to evolve the craft of senior living sales. We want to make the customer the center of the story, not the product. A more heroic, engaging sales process is needed to help prospects get emotionally ready to buy. We are no longer limited to shallow call-outs, superficial prospect relationships, and mediocre sales conversion rates.

> With PCS, we want to evolve the craft of senior living sales. We want to make the customer the center of the story, not the product.

PCS offers a field-tested shift in thinking that is supported by an evidence-based, theoretical model and corroborated by results and hard data.

Here's an update on Mary, one of those higher-functioning prospects. With our guidance, Mary got ready, made her own decision, and moved in. Six months later, she had a new partner, an improved relationship with her family, an active social life, and a Mediterranean cruise planned. She said, "I wish I had moved sooner!" Mary's daughter, her senior living sales counselor, the counselor's sales manager, the VP of sales, and the investors all have the same perspective.

We figured out how to lease the last 50 apartments at The Gatesworth in just 90 days. We did it by changing our sales paradigm and then our approach. We began spending more time with fewer prospects. We treated each one as someone special who needed help to overcome emotional resistance. It worked for us, and it can work for you. You can improve your sales effectiveness substantially. Faster fills and higher occupancies boost NOI as well as overall asset valuation.

You can help more senior adults get ready. Make it personal! Support your sales team's attempts to make it personal. Transactional selling has a significant negative impact on revenues. It misses out on serving over 90 percent of qualified prospects, namely those who are not forced to move due to a crisis. This outdated sales methodology continues to generate low occupancies, slow fills, shorter length of stay, and a high-acuity resident base. You can do better!

PCS improves sales effectiveness by focusing on what's behind our prospects' very personal decision-making journeys. Focus on their personal emotional barriers, namely fear of change. A PCS sales methodology accounts for the developmental stages of older adults. It also addresses the psychological principles of ambivalence, motivational interviewing, and stages of readiness to change.

I have spent most of the past 30 years heroically trying to understand what intentions and sales behaviors can help prospects who are "not ready yet" pivot emotionally in a way that allows many more of them to choose to move toward a better, longer, and more fulfilling life.

Guiding prospects to make a logical, reasoned decision that serves their best interests requires strategies and tactics designed to help them confront and hopefully overcome these deep-seated emotional barriers. I know because I have spent most of the past 30 years heroically trying to understand what intentions and sales behaviors can help prospects who are "not ready yet" pivot emotionally in a way that allows many more of them to choose to move toward a better, longer, and more fulfilling life.

Here are the highlights:

- **Connect:** Building trust with empathic connections opens up the opportunity for the prospect to be more responsive to untangling their emotional resistance.
- **Untangle:** Motivate and guide prospects as they try to grapple with their strong fears and resistance.
- **Advance:** There is a four-quadrant senior living navigational map that helps identify common stages of readiness for change. You can and should advance prospects through the continuum with short steps, always focused on increasing their readiness to make a logic-based buying decision.
- **Supporting data:** Count what counts toward driving higher sales conversions. We now have some ways of quantifying discovery, trust building, and readiness for change. More TSZ with fewer prospects drives better results. So does more planning, CFUs, home visits, and prospect photos.

Our intention is to change the way our industry sells. We have faced an uphill battle for acceptance. With this wave of new development and fierce completion and with most providers still struggling to gain occupancy with typical transactional or speed-to-lead approaches, PCS is gaining traction. If you are in the senior living industry, come join our movement. It will benefit you, your community, your company, and, most importantly, higher-functioning prospects like Mary, Mitch, Fred, and Rose and their

Together we can take steps to elevate sales in the senior living industry—heroic steps that will help our sales teams enhance the lives of tens of thousands more senior adults!

families. Together we can take steps to elevate sales in the senior living industry—heroic steps that will help our sales teams enhance the lives of tens of thousands more senior adults!

ACKNOWLEDGMENTS

My heartfelt appreciation and thanks to:

Alex Fisher, co-founder and president of Sherpa. For over 20 years, Alex has taught me a lot about connection, trust, and empathy. We filled a lot of difficult turnaround communities, side by side in the trenches. She collaborated with me to create and teach the change model behind Prospect-Centered Selling. Alex inspired both the creation of Sherpa and my writing of this book.

Charlie Deutsch, Bob Leonard, and Elana Spitzberg, my partners in the development and management of The Gatesworth communities. Starting from a person-centered, resident-first culture in 1988, we have worked, grown, and learned together for over 32 years.

Industry colleagues, especially Margaret Wylde, Dave Schless, Jim Moore, and the late Tony Mullen, for their collaboration and openness to sharing insights with me over several decades. Also, for their leadership in the quest for an evidence-based approach to senior living sales and for being industry pioneers who research, teach, and publish effective sales performance theory and data.

Pedro Soares, Sherpa CEO, and each of our amazing Sherpa leadership team members (past and present), investors, and incredible associates. With the growth of Sherpa, Prospect-Centered Selling has been able to morph from analog to digital, to scale, and to collect and analyze sales-related data. Sherpa is an incredible SaaS-based sales enablement platform that reflects and supports Prospect-Centered Selling with innovative CRM functionality, workflows, PCS sales training, and meaningful sales performance analytics.

Jonathan Levey and Dennis Schoen for their extraordinary personal contributions to three very successful turnaround campaigns with communities that we partnered on.

Frank Fisher from Sherpa for helping me edit my early drafts and the Scribe team for their guidance, motivation, tools, and oversight in getting my book published.

Finally, blessings to my children, Erica Spitzberg Smith and Aaron Spitzberg Smith; my grand-daughters, Emily, Ellie, Sophie, and Simone; and my bonus children, Francisco Fisher, Anya Fisher, and Amber Fisher, for their unconditional love and for the joy and inspiration they give me! I look forward to growing old with each one of you.

ABOUT THE AUTHOR

David Smith has reinvented himself several times in his life. After graduating from the prestigious Washington University School of Law, he practiced for 10 years before moving into the senior housing industry, where he acted as co-owner, developer, and manager of The Gatesworth at One McKnight Place and Parc Provence Memory Care. Both communities have been nationally recognized for innovation and quality services.

Following a successful fill-up of those properties, David founded a consulting business called One On One to provide marketing and sales assessments, training, and coaching to the senior housing industry. Along the way, he was recognized as the lead instructor first at Johns Hopkins and later at the Erickson School for Aging Sales and Marketing Programs. Through his presentations and peer-reviewed publications, David has built an outstanding reputation as a senior living industry thought leader.

In 2014, David pivoted again, joining partner Alexandra Fisher to bring the theory and science of Prospect-Centered Selling to life through a SaaS-based CRM and sales enablement platform called Sherpa. His life's work is to help older adults navigate the emotional obstacles associated with making a move in a respectful, compassionate way. He loves spending time in the sales office and ensures Sherpa stays fresh, current, and focused on meeting the needs of prospects first.

David is a father, grandfather, bonus dad, and Big Brother. He is an Eagle Scout who was named to an All-American high school water polo team. He graduated from Lake Forest College with a Phi Betta Kappa and National Handball Championship Team title. He served on the executive committee of the UJA National Leadership Cabinet and on the board of the St. Louis Jewish Federation.

CPSIA information can be obtained
at www.ICGtesting.com
Printed in the USA
BVHW070446090621
609068BV00004B/14/J